THE *Kingdom* OF *God* IS AT *Hand*

Alice Mims

The Kingdom of God Is at Hand

Trilogy Christian Publishers A Wholly Owned Subsidary of Trinity Broadcasting Network

2442 Michelle Drive Tustin, CA 92780

For information about special discounts for bulk purchases, please contact Trilogy Christian Publishing.

Trilogy Disclaimer: The views and content expressed in this book are those of the author and may not necessarily reflect the views and doctrine of Trilogy Christian Publishing or the Trinity Broadcasting Network.

Manufactured in the United States of America

10 9 8 7 6 5 4 3 2 1

Library of Congress Cataloging-in-Publication Data is available.

ISBN: 978-1-68556-446-9

E-ISBN: 978-1-68556-447-6

Dedication

This book is dedicated to the Lord My God, whose kingdom and righteousness I shall seek after all the days of my life, giving Him honor and praise while humbly sharing with others.

The Cherry Blossom Tree

What treasures you find from observing it; to set your eyes on it, you can see that the bloom of the flower on the tree is astonishingly beautiful and its color nurturing. You are fascinated by it.

The flowers that bloom are the fruit/gift of the tree and you might have also noticed that these flowers have a short life expectancy, but it can be renewed - how precious the flower is. In regards to you, like the flower wherever you are in this world, you add beauty/your fruit; in your time/season you bloom. If you were to touch this flower or touch your face with its petals, there is a good chance that you might get a hint of how you will feel in Heaven - an unexplainable, wonderful, overwhelming feeling of peace and joy, simultaneously. Change has happened in the world and the Holy Spirit brings your attention back to God; like The Cherry Blossom Tree - you can be renewed, born again, you have hope. God has made a way for you to come back to Him - through His son Jesus by His death on the cross. Your life is very precious to God. He wants you to know as He states in His Word, using the tree as a parable - for anything to truly matter, and to escape the destiny of this world (you need Him).

" I am the vine, ye are the branches: He that abideth in me, and I in him, the same bringeth forth much fruit: for without me ye can do nothing" (John 15:5).

Table of Contents

Introduction

This book is a must-read; it will show you the very heart of God, inspire you to want to know even the glorious, deep things of God, and you will experience great timeless stories that are food for thought, with powerfully delicious golden nuggets written down.

Inspired by God

"Seek ye the Lord while he may be found, call ye upon him while he is near" (Isaiah 55:6).

Preface

Why Should We Seek God Now?

God says, "I love them that love me; and those that seek me early shall find me" (Proverbs 8:17).

God/the Lord informs us in His Word, "And the Lord said unto Satan, Whence comest thou? Then Satan answered the Lord, and said, From going to and fro in the earth, and from walking up and down in it" (Job 1:7). God does not want us to give way to the devil (Satan) because he is evil; we should never trust him. As we see, God in His Word tells us that Satan is evil and is our enemy; he walks the earth. Satan is also known as the thief; God wants us to know that this thief (Satan) is amongst the earth, and what do thieves do? The Holy Spirit says God does not want you blind to the truth, the thief—he aims to steal your hope in the Persons of God (the truth), your calling/purpose, your gifts/talents, your joy, your peace, your health, your soul, your life, and so much more. God says if you know what Satan's plan is, then there is a good chance that you would come to the knowledge of the truth, that God is the only One who is more than able to fight against the enemy and win. God says, the enemy who is: "The thief cometh not, but for to steal, and to kill, and to destroy: I come that they might have life, and that they might have it more abundantly" (John 10:10). God wants us to know,

> There is one body, and one Spirit, as ye are called in one hope of your calling; one Lord, one faith, one baptism, one God and Father of all, who is above all, and through all, and in you all. But unto every one of us is given grace according to the measure of the gift of Christ. Wherefore he saith, When he ascended up on high, he led captivity captive and gave gifts unto men. (Now that he ascended, what is it but that he also descended first into the lower parts of the earth? He that descended is the same also that ascended up far above all heavens, that he might fill all things.) And he gave some apostles; and some, prophets; and some, evangelists; and some, pastors and teachers; For the perfecting of the saints, for the work of the ministry, for the edifying of the body of Christ: till we come in the unity of the faith, and of the knowledge of the Son of God, unto a perfect man, unto the measure

of the stature of the fullness of Christ: That we henceforth be no more children, tossed to and fro, and carried about with every wind of doctrine, by the sleight of men, and cunning craftiness, whereby they lie in wait to deceive; But speaking the truth in love, may grow up into him in all things, which is the head, even Christ: From whom the whole body fitly joined together and compacted by that which every joint supplieth, according to the effectual working in the measure of every part, maketh increase of the body unto the edifying of itself in love.

Ephesians 4:4–16

The Holy Spirit says, "For I will not have My children ignorant to the truth; the cries of My children I will not ignore, and I will help those who seek/cry out to Me, with all their heart. Amen." "For he saith, I have heard thee in a time accepted, and in the day of salvation have I succored thee: behold, now is the accepted time; behold, now is the day of salvation" (2 Corinthians 6:2).

May You Accompany Me,

on a Surprisingly Fulfilling Journey

into the Shekinah Presence of God

"As soon as Jesus heard the word that was spoken, he saith unto the ruler of the synagogue, Be not afraid, only believe" (Mark 5:36). "Let not your heart be troubled: ye believe in God, believe also in me" (John 14:1).

Why Is Life So Important?

Life is so important because life is the very breath of God in us, and with each breath we take, there is an opportunity/a chance for us to actually be and do what God originally intended for us. Amen.

What Is Hope?

The future is priceless; it is something to very much look forward to. Why? Because the future is where hope is. Hope is amazing; it is supernatural even. No matter what the day brings, we all have this in common: the future. We can be excited about our future because of hope. Hope is in Jesus Christ, the Lord, who came to give us the abundance of life. He is the One True God who is on our side, and when we choose Him, He holds our future in His hands. Come now, and let us hope in the future together.

> By whom also we have access by faith into
> this grace wherein we stand, and rejoice in
> hope of the glory of God. And not so, but

we glory in tribulations also: knowing that tribulation worketh patience; And patience, experience; and experience, hope: And hope maketh not ashamed; because the love of God is shed abroad in our hearts by the Holy Ghost which is given unto us.

Romans 5:2–5

"For we are saved by hope: but hope that is seen is not hope: for what a man seeth, why doth he yet hope for" (Romans 8:24)? "Jesus saith unto him, If thou canst believe, all things are possible to him that believeth" (Mark 9:23). "Blessed is the man that trusteth in the Lord, and whose hope the Lord is" (Jeremiah 17:7). Again, "The thief cometh not, but for to steal, and to kill, and to destroy: I come that they might have life, and that they might have it more abundantly" (John 10:10). Amen.

Golden Nugget

- How do we know we need something when we do not even know we need it? We know we need something when we are never satisfied. I've seen that the Word of God satisfies.

Let Us Pray...

We cry, Abba/Father, thank You for your unfailing love; forgive us and cleanse us from every known and unknown sin that we have done. Lord, please, help us not to do it again. For every breath we take, for every morning we wake, for every moment of every hour, for every second we live, it is by Your breath in us; we live because You allow it.

Oh, Father, touch us now with Your power and by Your might, to cleanse us, through and through, healing us of every unclean, any unrighteous, and anything that is not meant for our good, restoring us to our original intent by which You created us for, that we may prosper and be in good health, as our soul prospers. Give us a right spirit and a pure heart that we may surrender to You. Help us to follow You all the days of our life, to bring You honor and glory, in Jesus' name. We know that everything must obey Jesus. We thank You, for you are God Almighty. We know that this is Your will for us to pray—You always want the best for us; there is nothing too hard for You; we call on You, and we say it is done. Amen.

"And this is the confidence that we have in him, that, if we ask anything according to his will, he heareth us: and if we know that he hear us, whatsoever we ask, we know that we have the petitions that we desired of him" (1 John 5:14–15). "Let thy mercy, O Lord, be upon us, according as we hope in thee" (Psalm 33:22). "He sent his word, and healed them, and delivered them from their destructions" (Psalm 107:20). Amen.

Golden Nugget

- "And it shall come to pass in the last days, saith God, I will pour out of my Spirit upon all flesh: and your sons and your daughters shall prophesy, and your young men shall see visions, and your old men shall dream dreams" (Acts 2:17).

Chapter 1

Just as You Are!

Some will say that they must prepare to know/meet God. God wants us to be willing to believe that God *is* able to receive us just as we are. He is calling on us to stop making excuses/delaying forming a personal relationship with Him. God has already provided everything needed for us to be with Him. We must understand that God knows, and He cares for us; you can come to Him just as you are. For when we were still in sin, God came to save us. God gave us Jesus (His Son), "For he hath made him to be sin for us, who knew no sin; that we might be made the righteousness of God in him" (2 Corinthians 5:21).

> For I delivered unto you first of all that which I also received, how that Christ died for our sins according to the scriptures; and that he was buried, and that he rose again the third day according to the scriptures: and that he was seen of Cephas, then of the twelve: after that, he was seen of above five hundred brethren at once; of whom the

greater part remain unto this present, but some are fallen asleep.

1 Corinthians 15:3–6

"But God commendeth his love toward us, in that, while we were yet sinners, Christ died for us. For if, when we were enemies, we were reconciled to God by the death of his Son, much more, being reconciled, we shall be saved by his life" (Romans 5:8, 10). "Who will have all men to be saved, and to come unto the knowledge of the truth" (1 Timothy 2:4). "There hath no temptation taken you but such as is common to man: but God is faithful, who will not suffer you to be tempted above that ye are able; but will with the temptation also make a way to escape, that ye may be able to bear it" (1 Corinthians 10:13). "For God sent not his Son into the world to condemn the world; but that the world through him might be saved" (John 3:17). "For the Son of man is come to save that which was lost" (Matthew 18:11). "Come now, and let us reason together, saith the Lord: though your sins be as scarlet, they shall be as white as snow; though they be red like crimson, they shall be as wool" (Isaiah 1:18).

If we are weak or just a mess, God says, My strength is made perfect in your weakness, and I, the Lord your God, can take your mess and make it a masterpiece! We can never be so messed up that God is not able to save us. "And he said unto me, My grace is sufficient for thee: for my strength is made perfect in weakness. Most gladly therefore will I rather glory in my infirmities, that the power of Christ may rest upon me" (2 Corinthians 12:9). God comforts us by saying, "Take my yoke upon you, and learn of me; for I am meek and lowly in heart: and ye shall find rest unto your souls. For my yoke is easy, and my burden is light" (Matthew 11:29–30). Be assured that God is for you and not against you. God's intentions are always in your best interest. "For I know the thoughts that I think toward you, saith the Lord, thoughts of peace, and not of evil, to give you an expected end" (Jeremiah 29:11). Amen.

God thinks so much about us. He says, "There may be someone who looks a lot like you; there may be someone who talks in a way that you do; there may be someone who acts somewhat like you; there may even be someone who walks like you, but you are so amazing." God saw fit to make only one of you! There will never be two of you; there will never be another you. Go phenomenal You.

My Prayer for You...

Holy are You Lord God Almighty (our Father) in heaven; humbly I ask if You would, by Your grace, open the eyes of the heart, to give understanding to the one who hears/ reads what is within the pages of this book, that they may have great hope, Your peace that passes all understanding,

Your unmatched joy, be in health, and that they may know your unwavering agape love—that is only found in You (for Your glory) in Jesus' name. Amen.

Lord, How Will We Know the Way to Go?

The Word of God says, "Call unto me, and I will answer thee, and shew thee great and mighty things, which thou knowest not" (Jeremiah 33:3). God wants us to know that He will lead and guide us when we trust in Him. "He shall call upon me, and I will answer him: I will be with him in trouble; I will deliver him, and honour him" (Psalm 91:15). "I will instruct thee and teach thee in the way which thou shalt go: I will guide thee with mine eye" (Psalm 32:8).

Golden Nuggets

- We cannot change what has already happened, but we can learn from it.

- We do not get to choose where we came from, but we do get to choose where we are going.

- We do not become what someone says we are; we become who we were meant to be.

- Sometimes the end of a thing is far better than the beginning of it. Amen.

Chapter 2

THE *Kingdom* OF *God* IS AT *Hand*

The Kingdom of God Is at Hand!

Mark states, "And saying, The time is fulfilled, and the kingdom of God is at hand: repent ye, and believe the gospel" (Mark 1:15).

What Does This Mean?

This means the kingdom of God, which is within you, is close/near to you. The knowledge, wisdom, understanding, and authority from God are within your reach. You can know the will of God now. God's will shall be done now. God's will is available now. God's will is for us to turn from our ways/repent now. God's will is to seek Him now. Everything that pertains to godliness can be obtained now!

"Whether of them twain did the will of his father? They say unto him, The first. Jesus saith unto them, Verily I say unto you, That the publicans and the harlot go into the kingdom of God before you" (Matthew 21:31). And they repented not. "Neither shall they say, Lo here! or, lo there! for, behold, the kingdom of God is within you" (Luke 17:21). The Holy Spirit says, "And those which went before are without true understanding." God, "Who hath delivered us from the power of darkness, and hath translated us into the kingdom of his dear Son" (Colossians 1:13). For the believers of Jesus Christ, "He answered and said unto them, Because it is given unto you to know the mysteries of the kingdom of heaven, but to them it is not given" (Matthew 13:11). "If we say that we have no sin, we deceive ourselves, and the truth is not in us" (1 John 1:8). Therefore, the mystery of the kingdom of heaven is not given to those who do not repent because there's no truth in sin. To those who do not repent/turn from their own ways, but to those who truly repent and accept Jesus Christ as your Lord and Savior, then, "And he said, Unto you it is given to know the mysteries of the kingdom of God: but to others in parables; that seeing they might not see, and hearing they might not understand" (Luke 8:10).

The Holy Spirit says it is through Jesus, His righteousness, that all believers/in Christ shall know the mysteries of the kingdom of heaven and the kingdom of God. God wants to rescue/save those that are lost. Amen.

What Does It Mean to Repent?

The Holy Spirit says to repent means to completely turn from your ways, to wholeheartedly stop doing things that are against God's will.

How Do You Repent?

"If we confess our sins, he is faithful and just to forgive us our sins, and to cleanse us from all unrighteousness" (1 John 1:9). "But if we walk in the light, as he is in the light, we have fellowship one with another, and the blood of Jesus Christ his Son cleanseth us from all sin" (1 John 1:7). "He that saith he is in the light, and hateth his brother, is in darkness even until now" (1 John 2:9). In other words, in order to repent, we must, in our hearts, without doubt, want to turn from our own ways and want more than anything to trust in God totally. We also must accept the Son of God, who is Jesus. As we see above, He is the only One because of His shed blood that can cleanse us from all sin.

Why Must We Repent?

We must repent because God does not want us to perish! When you repent, you turn the face of God toward you. In order to be forgiven so that God will help us, we must repent; God does not condone sin, God cannot sin, and He has nothing to do with sin. If we do not repent of sin first, God will not respond to our prayers. Not repenting, we stop the hand of God from moving on our behalf. Even unconfessed sin that stays hidden in our hearts hinders our prayers. This is why God says to confess the sin, that it will be removed from our hearts.

We cannot speak out of our mouth one thing and yet not mean what we say in our hearts, because if we do this, we are fools to think that God does not see the contents of our heart; God cannot be fooled! Therefore, God tells us what the right way to come to Him is; it is by repentance. If we obey God and truly repent of our sins, He will have mercy on us. God says, "For I will be merciful to their unrighteousness, and their sins and their iniquities will I remember no more" (Hebrews 8:12).

As we see above, sin blocks you from receiving from God; please do not sin. Repenting allows you to come into the presence of God! Our prayers cannot be answered if sin is not repented of, which includes but is not limited to unforgiveness in your heart. Ask for God's forgiveness and apologize for what you have done wrong. For whatever you have done, and whatever you will do, for whatever it might be, it does not matter; as long as you are truly remorseful, God will forgive you. He says He has need of you, yes, you. Unforgiveness blocks your blessings! If you truly do not forgive first, before you repent, then how can you be forgiven by God? When you forgive, I mean truly forgive, there are three parts to forgiving: 1) you must want to forgive; 2) do the forgiving (forgive), and; 3) in order for the forgiveness to work, then you must—whatever you are forgiving—let it go. Ask for God's help if you cannot truly forgive. "The Lord is not slack concerning his promise, as some men count slackness; but is longsuffering to us-ward, not willing that any should perish, but that all should come to repentance" (2 Peter 3:9). "I tell you, Nay: but, except ye repent, ye shall all likewise perish" (Luke 13:3). God also says, "And be ye kind one to another, tenderhearted, forgiving one another, even as God for Christ's sake hath forgiven you" (Ephesians 4:32). "But as he which hath called you is holy, so be ye holy in all manner of conversation; because it is written, Be ye holy; for I am holy" (1 Peter 1:15–16).

How Can I Be Holy as God Says I Should Be? What Must I Do to Be Holy?

"By the which will we are sanctified through the offering of the body of Jesus Christ once for all" (Hebrews

10:10). To be holy, we must "Be therefore followers of God, as dear children" (Ephesians 5:1). The Holy Spirit says we must meditate on God's Word day and night; we must trust in God completely and be careful to do God's will. For example, forgive, pursue peace with all men, guard your heart, mind the way of your words, resist the devil, be baptized of the Father, of the Son, of the Holy Ghost in the Name of Jesus; set yourself apart from the world for the glory of God, watch and pray, always. To follow in this manner, which is stated above, This is holy, says the Lord.

Jesus says, "Go ye therefore, and teach all nations, baptizing them in the name of the Father, and of the Son, and of the Holy Ghost" (Matthew 28:19). "And whatsoever ye shall ask in my name, that will I do, that the Father may be glorified in the Son" (John 14:13). "And fear not them which kill the body, but are not able to kill the soul: but rather fear him which is able to destroy both soul and body in hell" (Matthew 10:28). "But I will forewarn you whom ye shall fear: Fear him, which after he hath killed hath power to cast into hell; yea, I say unto you, Fear him" (Luke 12:5). "Hitherto have ye asked nothing in my name: ask, and ye shall receive, that your joy may be full" (John 16:24). "But your iniquities have separated between you and your God, and your sins have hid his face from you, that he will not hear" (Isaiah 59:2).

> If we say that we have no sin, we deceive
> ourselves, and the truth is not in us. If we
> confess our sins, he is faithful and just to
> forgive us our sins, and to cleanse us from
> all unrighteousness. If we say that we have
> not sinned, we make him a liar, and his
> word is not in us.

1 John 1:8–10

"Who shall ascend into the hill of the Lord? or who shall stand in his holy place? He that hath clean hands and a pure heart; who hath not lifted up his soul unto vanity, nor sworn deceitfully" (Psalm 24:3–4). "Can any hide himself in secret places that I shall not see him? Do not I fill heaven and earth? saith the Lord" (Jeremiah 23:24). "For if ye forgive men their trespasses, your heavenly Father will also forgive you: but if ye forgive not men their trespasses, neither will your Father forgive your trespasses" (Matthew 6:14–15).

Let us take a look in the Holy Bible about Moses and the burning bush, as this story relates to what the Holy Spirit has instructed me to write in the passages above what we've just read. Why did God appear to Moses in the burning bush, and why wasn't the bush consumed by the fire of God? God appeared to Moses in the burning bush to speak to him, and He said, "Thou canst not see my face: for there shall no man see me, and live" (Exodus 33:20). God had seen the suffering and heard the cries of His people; God told Moses to bring His people/children of Israel out of Egypt. "And he said, Draw not nigh hither: put off thy shoes from off thy feet, for the place whereon thou standest is holy ground" (Exodus 3:5). I'll tell you a secret: when God appeared to Moses in the burning bush, the bush was not consumed by the fire of God because the bush had no sin; it was God's holiness. He did not command for it to be destroyed; instead, since no man can see God face to face and live, God used the burning bush to speak, get the attention of Moses, show and exemplify His power, which is only found in Him (God) so that Moses might be encouraged to do His will.

> For the scripture saith unto Pharaoh, Even for this same purpose have I raised thee up, that I might shew my power in thee, and that my name might be declared throughout all the earth. Therefore, hath he mercy on whom he will have mercy, and whom he will he hardeneth. Thou wilt say then unto me, Why doth he yet find fault? For who

hath resisted his will? Nay but, O man, who art thou that repliest against God? Shall the thing formed say to him that formed it, Why hast thou made me thus? Hath not the potter power over the clay, of the same lump to make one vessel unto honour, and another unto dishonour?

Romans 9:17–21

In other words, God was making it clear to Moses that in order to do His will, God Himself would raise Moses to get the attention of the pharaoh, and God said everything is all in His hands, that He will have mercy on whom He pleases. To any or to those who resist God's will, He shall find fault with them. God says, for which He made mankind, there will be no question pertaining to the power of God over all things, and He shall divide His creation into two parts, the just/righteous and the unjust/unrighteous. This is the will of God. The Holy Spirit has continued to instruct me, to reify that we can be in the presence of God but not see His face in our current body state and live— that is another story we will not explore right now. But God also said that we might stand in the shadow of God and live. As you probably already know, "He that dwelleth in the secret place of the Most High shall abide under the shadow of the Almighty" (Psalm 91:1).

Golden Nugget

- No one can refute the immutable Word of God.

Chapter 3

Why Should God Be Obeyed?

We should obey God because He that knows the end from the beginning must be obeyed!

"Declaring the end from the beginning and from ancient times the things that are not yet done, saying, My counsel shall stand, and I will do all my pleasure" (Isaiah 46:10). Fear God and keep His commandments. God is great, and He is worthy to be praised! I heard a man say, "God's creation speaks for Him." In other words, the wonder of God's creation is great. Therefore, again I will say, God is great, and greatly, He should be praised! Amen. "Great is the Lord, and greatly to be praised, and his greatness is unsearchable" (Psalm 145:3). "The earth is the Lord's, and the fullness thereof; the world, and they that dwell therein" (Psalm 24:1). "Let us hear the conclusion of the whole matter. Fear God, and keep his commandments: for this is the whole duty of man" (Ecclesiastes 12:13).

Golden Nugget

- For those who love God, it is refreshing to see that when you have gotten everything all figured out (or so you think), then God steps in and turns everything in a whole different direction. The best thing about God intervening in our plans is that He is always in our best interest, and He knows the best thing for us, even if we cannot see it. Amen.

Chapter 4

What Is the Kingdom of God, and Why Should We Know about This?

The kingdom of God is God within you, God/the Holy Spirit living on the inside of you. "Neither shall they say, Lo here! or, lo there! for, behold, the kingdom of God is within you" (Luke 17:21). "For the kingdom of God is not meat and drink; but righteousness, and peace, and joy in the Holy Ghost" (Romans 14:17). The kingdom of God can only be seen and understood by choosing Jesus (God's Son).

It is imperative that we know about the kingdom of God for three reasons: God loves us, and He cares for us so much that He invests Himself in us and communicates His love for us with grace and mercy toward us. We are of utmost importance to God. Why is this? *First reason*: God has said He placed His kingdom in us, which is incomparable to Him. Amen.

What Does God Say Is the Most Important Part of a Person Besides His Soul? Do You Know?

Mankind is unprecedented and incredibly designed. *Second reason*: the most important part of a person is our spirit. Why? Because our spirit is God's light, which He has placed in the core/center of our body. God has placed His light (which is the spirit of man) in every one of us. "But there is a spirit in man: and the inspiration of the Almighty giveth them understanding" (Job 32:8). "The spirit of man is the candle of the Lord, searching all the inward parts of the belly" (Proverbs 20:27). "The spirit of a man will sustain his infirmity; but a wounded spirit who can bear?" (Proverbs 18:14). "For ye are bought with a price: therefore glorify God in your body and in your spirit, which are God's" (1 Corinthians 6:20). "For we have not a high priest which cannot be touched with the feeling of our infirmities; but was in all points tempted like as we are yet without sin. Let us therefore come boldly unto the throne of grace, that we may obtain mercy, and find grace to help in time of need" (Hebrews 4:15–16).

So that we're not confused, there is a difference between the spirit of man, which is the candle of the Lord, and the spirit man/inner man/inward man, which is our spiritual body. "We will get better acquainted with our spirit man/spiritual body in the upcoming chapters," says the Holy Spirit.

God wants us to know all these things because He does not want us to be ignorant of the truth. He does not want us to die; He wants us to know that we can come to Him and that He can be reached. He wants to be included in our lives. God is approachable and relational to His creation because He loves us and enjoys our company. God says we are created in His image, after His likeness, and we are wonderfully made. Ask yourself this, Would you care and protect or want to be in relations with something you created or made that was wonderful? Would that be pleasing to you?

God watches over His own. "The Lord shall preserve thy going out and thy coming in from this time forth, and even for evermore" (Psalm 121:8). God is great. "I will praise thee; for I am fearfully and wonderfully made: marvelous are thy works; and that my soul knoweth right well" (Psalm 139:14). In order for us to see this and fully understand it, we must know the personality and character of God the Father. God is love, sovereign, righteous, the judge, full of grace, and holy. It is through Jesus Christ, our Lord, that God lowered His divinity to save us. God wants us to have knowledge, wisdom, understanding, and to know the truth so that we might choose to be with what is best for us. Ultimately, God is best for us, and He does not want us to live without the truth and be dammed for

41

eternity because we are without God.

God has given us another gift, and this gift is the power to choose our eternity. God says so that we might know the authentic importance of His purpose for us, which is to carry out His will together (with Him). God seeks to be the only One to reign over us/His creation. Amen. "And I heard a great voice out of heaven saying, Behold, the tabernacle of God is with men, and he will dwell with them, and they shall be his people, and God himself shall be with them and be their God" (Revelation 21:3). And God came down Himself, as Jesus, and said, "Thou madest him a little lower than the angels; thou crownedst him with glory and honour, and didst set him over the works of thy hands" (Hebrews 2:7). "But our God is in the heavens: he hath done whatsoever he hath pleased" (Psalm 115:3). "Whatsoever the Lord pleased, that did he in heaven, and in earth, in the seas, and all deep places" (Psalm 135:6). "And all the inhabitants of the earth are reputed as nothing: and doeth according to his will in the army of heaven, and among the inhabitants of the earth: and none can stay his hand, or say unto him, What doest thou" (Daniel 4:35)? "In whom also we have obtained an inheritance, being predestinated according to the purpose of him who worketh all things after the counsel of his own will" (Ephesians 1:11).

The *third reason*, "And God said, Let us make man in our image, after our likeness..." Later, we shall explore what is meant when God says, "Let us" make man in our image, after our likeness.

> So God created man in His own image, in the image of God created he him; male and female created he them. And God blessed them, and God said unto them, Be fruitful, and multiply, and replenish the earth, and subdue it: and have dominion over the fish of the sea, and over the fowl of the air, and over every living thing that moveth upon the earth.

Genesis 1:27–28

"And God saw everything that he had made, and, behold, it was very good. And the evening and the morning were the sixth day" (Genesis 1:31).

As we see, everything God made, He said it was good. We need not take that lightly because the scripture says that God is the only One who is good. Jesus said, "And he said unto him, Why callest thou me good? There is none good but one, that is God: but if thou wilt enter into life, keep the commandments" (Matthew 19:17). "For God so loved the world, that he gave his only begotten Son, that whosoever believeth in him should not perish, but have everlasting life" (John 3:16). God loves us so much that He gave to us His only Son, whom He loves and is well pleased with. Through His Son, we are saved. This shows us that we are invaluable to God. To think He would say everything He made was good—as we clearly see above, God Himself said, in His Word, that we were "made good/ we are well made," and we can see that we matter to Him dearly. Amen.

Golden Nugget

- Nothing is above the truth. Do you know the truth? "Jesus saith unto him, I am the way, the truth, and the life: no man cometh unto the Father, but by me" (John 14:6). "Sanctify them through thy truth: thy word is truth" (John 17:17).

Chapter 5

Character

Let's review the character/personality of God from my perspective!

What Does Character Mean to Me?

To me, "character" is our personal qualities or things that distinguish us as an individual, and "character" has an original starting point. Let us take a look at where character begins. I believe the original starting point of character in all of us begins with God. "And the Lord God formed man of the dust of the ground, and breathed into his nostrils the breath of life; and man became a living soul" (Genesis 2:7). "The spirit of God hath made me and the breath of the Almighty hath given me life" (Job 33:4).

The spirit of man is the candle of the Lord, in which the light of God in us shines through us, through our character/personality. The Holy Spirit says, "The spirit of man is the candle of the Lord, searching all the inward parts of the belly" (Proverbs 20:27). Character—He is awesome, and in His magnitude, He is astonishing!

What Does His Magnitude Mean?

I believe the magnitude of God's awesomeness towards us cannot be measured. I also believe God has placed some of His magnitude to be expressed in our character. Character is placed in all of us from the very start—character goes back to the thought of us when we were in the mind of God. Character is who we are, the core of us. It is the best part of us, given to us from the heart of God. To me, character goes real deep, inside of us, wanting to come out, through us, waiting to be noticed by us so that it can do what it was put in us to do: shine on wherever you are in the world. Our character shows how brilliant we are and how awesome God is in all of us. We must, through our life experiences, learn how to operate in our God-given character, to see our awesome God working at His magnitude through us, by our character. We will be judged by our character by God and by man. No one is satisfied completely until their character shines. Character is when you and God perform your purpose together, making you distinct. Character is a part of us, and He longs for us to know this. Character is from the heart of God and given to us by God. He wants to come out and come through us to do His amazing work on the earth.

Character is essential, and He is who we need to be truly happy in this world. Character is so grand because it's God's light shining through, helping us in our purpose.

He continually unfolds in us, shaping us into who we are meant to be. Character helps us to do, to hope. Character is a gift from God, given to all of us. It is up to you to accept Him and have the privilege to experience His full essence. Character is personalized; it is the way one thinks, acts, and does to his or her ability. All the above is how I define character, with the help of the Holy Spirit, of course. Therefore, be not deceived into underestimating the power of God in Christ through His chosen. "But we speak the wisdom of God in a mystery, even the hidden wisdom, which God ordained before the world unto our glory: Which none of the princes of this world knew: for had they known it, they would not have crucified the Lord of glory" (1 Corinthians 2:7–8). I believe our character, awakened and empowered by the Holy Spirit, helps us to have longevity, learn how to live in abundance, and will help us to turn from sin; everything relies on us keeping our character intact, which is from God. "Stay in your character regardless," says the Holy Spirit, "because you will be judged by man and by God accordingly." Amen.

God has said in His Word that there will come a time where we will not be able to seek God; therefore, God says now is the time to seek Him before it is too late so that our soul might be delivered from an eternal hell. As you know evil does exist, you must also know hell exists too, and God, who is full of grace and mercy, will spare every one of us from hell if we trust in Him with all our heart. He has communicated this repeatedly through His Word. The words in the Bible are true. The Lord says when all the scriptures are fulfilled, everything shall pass away except God's Word, and we are seeing His Word being fulfilled, which the prophets of God have said.

> And he said unto them, These are the words which I spake unto you, while I was yet with you, that all things must be fulfilled, which were written in the law of Moses, and in the prophets, and in the psalms, concerning me. Then opened he their understanding, that they might understand the scriptures.
>
> **Luke 24:44–45**

"Verily, I say unto you, This generation shall not pass, till all these things be fulfilled" (Matthew 24:34). "For verily I say unto you, Till heaven and earth pass, one jot or one tittle shall in no wise pass from the law, till all be fulfilled" (Matthew 5:18). "Heaven and earth shall pass away: but my words shall not pass away" (Mark 13:31). For the Lord God heard what man said,

> For that which I do I allow not: for what I would, that do I not; but what I hate, that do

I. If then I do that which I would not, I consent unto the law that it is good. Now then it
is no more I that do it, but sin that dwelleth
in me. For I know that in me (that is, in my
flesh,) dwelleth no good thing: for too will
is present with me; but how to perform that
which is good I find not. For the good that I
would I do not: but the evil which I would
not, that I do. Now if I do that I would not,
it is no more I that do it, but sin that dwelleth in me. I find then a law, that, when I
would do good, evil is present with me. For
I delight in the law of God after the inward
man: but I see another law in my members,
warring against the law of my mind, and
bringing me to captivity to the law of sin
which is in my members. O wretched man
that I am! who shall deliver me from the
body of this death?

Romans 7:15–24

To me, the Bible points out our lack of knowing; not
empowering our character leaves us unsettled within.

What Do the Scriptures Mean in Romans 7:15–24?
The Holy Spirit of God says that man has said, "I do

not understand why I do the things I do." When I know to do right, but I do not, I end up doing what I hate. By me doing what I am not supposed to do, I am consenting to this wrong already, which is the law of this world, calling it good when it is not. I know that I do not willingly do wrong, but it is the sin that is in me that takes over. As the scripture points out, there is no good thing from it (my flesh) because my flesh is against what is right. Sometimes there is a struggle because I know what is right and what I want to do right now, but I am not sure of how I should go about it. I continue to know what is good/right, but I also continue to do evil/wrong, which I do not want to do. I know that there is a law then, that when I would do good, evil is present with me. For I delight in the law of God, which the inward man/my spirit man loves, but I see another law, also in me, fighting against the law of my mind (to do good) and holding me captive to the law of sin, which is also in me. When I let sin take over, I am miserable, unhappy, never satisfied (continuously suffering) because of this sin, which leads to death! "For the wages of sin is death; but the gift of God is eternal life through Jesus Christ our Lord" (Romans 6:23). Who will "deliver me from the body of this death?" Jesus says, "I am the way, the truth, and the life" (John 14:6). I will deliver you! Seek me! Amen.

Golden Nugget

- Jesus says,

I have yet many things to say unto you, but ye cannot bear them now. Howbeit when he, the Spirit of truth, is come, he will guide you into all truth: for he shall not speak of himself; but whatsoever he shall hear, that shall he speak: and he will shew you things to come. He shall glorify me: for he shall receive of mine, and shall shew it unto you. All things that the Father hath are mine: therefore, said I, that he shall take of mine, and shall shew it unto you.

John 16:12–15

Chapter 6

Why Does God Say Guard/Renew Your Mind?

The Word of God says to renew our minds because with our spiritual mind, when we accept Jesus Christ, we are born again, better able to serve God. "For the weapons of our warfare are not carnal, but mighty through God to the pulling down of strongholds; casting down imaginations, and every high thing that exalteth itself against the knowledge of God, and bringing into captivity every thought to the obedience of Christ" (2 Corinthians 10:4–5). "Thou wilt keep him in perfect peace, whose mind is stayed on thee: because he trusteth in thee" (Isaiah 26:3). "Commit thy works unto the Lord, and thy thoughts shall be established" (Proverbs 16:3). "And be not conformed to this world: but be ye transformed by the renewing of your mind, that ye may prove what is that good, and acceptable, and perfect, will of God" (Romans 12:2). "Finally, brethren, whatsoever things are true, whatsoever things are pure, whatsoever things are lovely, whatsoever things are of good report; if there be any virtue, and if there be any praise, think on these things" (Philippians 4:8). Many things enter us through our mind; this is why we must renew it with the Word of God and guard our mind by monitoring what enters it. "I thank God through Jesus Christ our Lord. So then with the mind, I myself serve the law of God; but with the flesh, the law of sin" (Romans 7:25). God says, "For all have sinned, and come short of the glory of God" (Romans 3:23).

Sin came about a long time ago in the world and started in the Garden from the first man and woman created by God, who were called Adam and Eve. Through their disobedience to God, by them believing in the lies of the devil, our enemy, sin was manifested!

> Wherefore, as by one man sin entered into the world, and death by sin; and so death passed upon all men, for that all have sinned: (For until the law sin was in the world: but sin is not imputed when there is no law. Nevertheless, death reigned from Adam to Moses, even over them that had not sinned after the similitude of Adam's transgression, who is the figure of him that was to come. But not as the offense, so also is the free gift. For if through the offence of one many be dead, much more the grace of God, and the gift by grace, which is by one man, Jesus Christ, hath abounded unto

56

many. And not as it was by one that sinned, so is the gift: for the judgment was by one condemnation, but the free gift is of many offenses unto justification. For if by one man's offence death reigned by one; much more they which receive abundance of grace and of the gift of righteousness shall reign in life by one, Jesus Christ.)

Romans 5:12–17

"For as by one man's disobedience many were made sinners, so by the obedience of one shall many be righteous" (Romans 5:19). Know this, disobedience is sin, and sin leads to death.

What Is Death?

This is a question that many ask, but to this question, there is not just one answer for the explanation of it. This question has multiple answers because there are many deaths! For instance, there is a daily death—dying to sin daily, in other words, repenting often. There is dead to sin—that Christ might live in you. There is a physical death—when the body dies. There is spiritual death—when the spirit in you dies/sleeps, leaving you apart from God. There is the second death—a lake of fire. The Bible says, "And death and hell were cast into the lake of fire.

This is the second death" (Revelation 20:14).

Most people who ask, "What is death?" are referring to physical death. This is when the body dies because this is what they know. When one dies a physical death, it is not the end of all things, but the Holy Spirit says it is the beginning of eternity for the soul of the body of this person. All those feelings the dead person experienced while their body was alive, their soul after their body dies, they will experience intensified/immense feelings in eternity. Your beginning, after you die, ultimately is up to you! You will experience, with God in eternity, all that is good. For example, happiness, love, a perfect life after death with Christ our Lord. Or your beginning after you die will be extreme torment/suffering intensively, all the time for eternity with the devil—the unmerciful evil one! Now, this question remains to be answered by you: when your body dies, where will you spend your eternity? With Jesus Christ—would you like to know Him? Answering the original question— what is death? Death is not the absence of life; it is the beginning of eternity without your earthly body. Jesus said, "And whosoever liveth and believeth in me shall never die. Believest thou this" (John 11:26)? This is how you choose a perfect eternity, choose Jesus Christ our Lord, "That if thou shalt confess with thy mouth the Lord Jesus, and shalt believe in thine heart that God hath raised him from the dead, thou shalt be saved" (Romans 10:9). Amen.

Golden Nugget

- What life is, death is not!

What life gives, death cannot!

Life is Jesus Christ!

Choose to live in Christ.

"Jesus saith unto him, I am the way, the truth, and the life: no man cometh unto the Father, but by me" (John 14:6). Life is like a wrapped gift from God, waiting to be opened. Amen.

Chapter 7

Seek Me

My dear children, there is no joy in sorrow, but there is salvation in forgiveness, and there is no hope in what has already passed, but there is hope in your future. Therefore, true joy is being forgiven by God through Christ Jesus. The Lord says that great hope is "in *Me—the Lord God Almighty*, I am the future, Seek Me!"

We must look forward to the future and not live in the past. Always focusing on the past robs us of our future. "Brethren, I count not myself to have apprehended: but this one thing I do, forgetting those things which are behind, and reaching forth unto those things which are before, I press toward the mark for the prize of the high calling of God in Christ Jesus" (Philippians 3:13–14). Amen.

Golden Nuggets

- God said we must be discerning of our dreams and of those who speak into our future (prophesying),

- I have not sent these prophets, yet they ran: I have not spoken to them, yet they prophesied. But if they had stood in my counsel, and had caused my people to hear my words, then they should have turned them from their evil way, and from the evil of their doings. Am I a God at hand, saith the Lord, and not a God afar off? Can any hide himself in secret places that I shall not see him? saith the Lord. Do not I fill heaven and earth? saith the Lord. I have heard what the prophets said, that prophesy lies in my name, saying, I have dreamed, I have dreamed. How long shall this be in the heart of the prophets that prophesy lies? yea, they are prophets of the deceit of their own heart; Which think to cause my people to forget my name by their dreams which they tell every man to his neighbor, as their fathers have forgotten my name for Baal. The prophet that hath a dream, let him tell a dream; and he that hath my word, let him speak my word faithfully. What is the chaff to the wheat? saith the Lord.

Jeremiah 23:21–28

I heard the Holy Spirit say the chaff is the husk—the part that you can throw away. The wheat is the seed—the part we eat, meaning, in the scripture above, we may forget or discard the way we receive the Word, but to those who speak the Word of God, must speak in faith to plant God's Word, because it is the seed that we may eat, in order to live our expected end. Amen. "For I know the thoughts that I think toward you, saith the Lord, thoughts of peace, and not of evil, to give you an expected end" (Jeremiah 29:11).

- The Holy Spirit says dreams and visions are very important; they can make our future better if we pursue them. Our dreams can take us where we cannot physically go; our dreams show us what can become possible, and our dreams can give us hope for the future. Sometimes, God communicates with us through them. Dreams and visions are spiritual. God has made dreams and visions to benefit us. We need God's help in understanding them and bringing them to fruition.

- Do not just believe that the best is only in the future but also believe that the best can be for now, through Jesus Christ our Lord. How do we know when the dreams and visions are from God? "But he that prophesieth speaketh unto men to edification, and exhortation, and comfort" (1 Corinthians 14:3)

- And the Lord answered me, and said, Write the

vision, and make it plain upon tables, that he may run that readeth it. For the vision is yet for an appointed time, but at the end it shall speak, and not lie: though it tarry, wait for it; because it will surely come, it will not tarry.

Habakkuk 2:2–3

Amen.

Golden Nugget

- Wherever your treasure is (What you want or invest in the most), there is your heart also. The Holy Spirit instructs me to focus on eternity where God is because our days on earth are numbered.

Chapter 8

Why Do We Come Short?

To come short and fall short mean the same. We fall short because we refuse to follow the Word of God, or we sometimes misunderstand it, or we believe it is not true. Refusing the Word of God, misunderstanding the Word of God, or not believing the Word of God all equals coming/ falling short of the glory of God. If you are not for God, you are not following God; therefore, you sin, which is against God.

Why Must We Stay Away from Sin When It Feels Good?

Sin is the trick of the enemy; he knows that the flesh of a man/woman is weak and self-pleasing, so he looks for ways that will make you want to easily slip into sin, to fall into temptation. Therefore, you end up backsliding and turn from God without noticing. The enemy uses all kinds of devices to attack your life, such as drugs, illness, sexual perversions, your loved ones to turn against you, and the love of money, just to name a few. No matter how good doing bad feels, it is still sin; it deceives you because sin will never be for your benefit, and sin will never be good or right, even if it feels good. Our feelings are not truth; we should not rely on our feelings in our decision-making because they are always changing according to what is going on, but the Word of God is reliable. It changes not and has been proven successful when we fully trust in God.

We cannot trust man or ourselves because that is from our own understanding/heart and not God's. "He that trusteth in his own heart is a fool: but whoso walketh wisely, he shall be delivered" (Proverbs 28:26). "The way of a fool is right in his own eyes: but he that hearkeneth unto counsel is wise" (Proverbs 12:15). "There is a way which seemeth right unto a man, but the end thereof are the ways of death. Even in laughter the heart is sorrowful; and the end of that mirth is heaviness" (Proverbs 14:12–13). Trusting in our own hearts can be dangerous if we are not guided by God's Word and His Spirit. For example, if someone hurts you and you want to hurt them back, something terrible, because your heart is broken or your feelings are hurt deeply, it's not right to intentionally cause harm/pain on anyone. We cannot put all our trust in our own heart/feelings; we need God's guidance or someone who can help us to do right in some instances. "Wherefore seeing we also are compassed about with so great a cloud of witnesses, let us lay aside every weight, and the sin which doth so easily beset us, and let us run with patience the race that is set before us" (Hebrews 12:1).

The Holy Spirit says mankind has continued to decline morally; therefore, mankind must stop seeking after their own heart, and they must seek after every word that precedeth out of the mouth of God. "Having the understanding darkened, being alienated from the life of God through the ignorance that is in them, because of the blindness of their heart" (Ephesians 4:18). God said, therefore, we must "Watch and pray, that ye enter not into temptation: the spirit indeed is willing, but the flesh is weak" (Matthew 26:41). "Submit yourselves therefore to God. Resist the devil, and he will flee from you" (James 4:7). I have decisively considered the weight of sin (a few minutes of sinful pleasure) will lead to an eternity of torment in hell, so I shall therefore resist sin as God says, which is against God, stay away from it, and I will constantly submit/hold my flesh captive under the obedience of Jesus Christ my Lord. Amen.

Golden Nugget

- My soul is corrected by your tender Word, dear Lord, cast me not from Your presence, in You I do hope, and in Jesus' name, I pray. Amen. Just as the scriptures say, "Cast me not away from thy presence; and take not the holy spirit from me" (Psalm 51:11). "For the word of the Lord is right; and all his works are done in truth" (Psalm 33:4). "Order my steps in thy word: and let not any iniquity have dominion over me. Deliver me from the oppression of man: so will I keep thy precepts. Make thy face to shine upon thy servant, and teach me thy statutes" (Psalm 119:133–135). Amen.

Prayer of Repentance

May You please forgive me, Father, I have sinned against You, I now repent of my sin, please help me, Lord God, to hide Your Word in my heart, that I may not sin against You, in Jesus' name. Amen. I then find myself praying the Word of God in confidence, knowing that He hears me and He helps me always because His Word says that; I also know God's Word speaks and does. Amen. "And this is the confidence that we have in him, that, if we ask anything according to his will, he heareth us: and if we know that he hear us, whatsoever we ask, we know that we have the petitions that we desired of him" (1 John 5:14–15). "Thy word have I hid in my heart, that I might not sin against thee" (Psalm 119:11). "Shew me thy ways, O Lord; teach me thy paths. Lead me in thy truth, and teach me: for thou art the God of my salvation; on thee do I wait all the day" (Psalm 25:4–5). In Jesus' name, I pray. Amen.

Why Did I Say "In Jesus' Name"?

Because God says that it is through His Son Jesus that He helps us, that His death is not in vain. "And whatsoever ye do in word or deed, do all in the name of the Lord Jesus, giving thanks to God and the Father by him" (Colossians 3:17). Amen. Let us look at what apostle Paul is saying in the scriptures, "To whom ye forgive anything, I forgive also: for if I forgave anything, to whom I forgave it, for your sakes forgave I it in the person of Christ; lest Satan should get an advantage of us: for we are not ignorant of his devices" (2 Corinthians 2:10–11).

We must ask God to help us forgive, that we may forgive in righteousness if we do not forgive through Jesus Christ, I find then another law, not of God, but it is of the devil. The devil hates mankind so much that he corrupts the natural/original intent/order of a person or thing, calling it good when it is not. The law of the devil is to make what is holy/sacred defiled/unholy. "For we wrestle not against flesh and blood, but against principalities, against powers, against the rulers of the darkness of this world, against spiritual wickedness in high places" (Ephesians 6:12). God says we must, therefore, put on the whole armor of God to stand against spiritual wickedness in high places.

"Faith"

"For unto us was the gospel preached, as well as unto them: but the word preached did not profit them, not being mixed with faith in them that heard it" (Hebrews 4:2).

Chapter 9

What Is the Armor of God?

Why do we need it? How do we put it on? How to use it? And what are the eight principles of the armor of God? The whole armor of God is most powerful. It is the armor that Jesus wore when He walked the earth as man and God, so you can count on its reliability. The Lord says that He, the Holy One of Israel, has given you power. "Death and life are in the power of the tongue: and they that love it shall eat the fruit thereof" (Proverbs 18:21). "For by Him were all things created, that are in heaven, and that are in earth, visible and invisible, whether they be thrones, or dominions, or principalities, or powers: all things were created by him, and for him" (Colossians 1:16). The armor is God's spoken Word, which is the righteousness of Jesus Christ applied to our life, carried out by believing and enforcing having faith.

Which Exists, the Visible World/Realm/Domain or the Invisible World/Realm/Domain?

They both exist, as we see in the scripture above.

The visible and the invisible both exist on the earth simultaneously.

Which Is Dominant, the Visible or the Invisible?

The invisible is dominant. Why? As the scripture reads, this is the eternal place that cannot die. There are principalities or powers that rule in high places—you cannot see with your physical eyes. The invisible realm is dominant and most powerful because of God, who is Spirit; His throne exists there. We know that the things we see are made by the things we cannot see. "Through faith, we understand that the worlds were framed by the word of God so that things which are seen were not made of things which do appear" (Hebrews 11:3). Jesus, "Who is the image of the invisible God, the firstborn of every creature" (Colossians 1:15). "While we look not at the things which are seen, but at the things which are not seen: for the things which are seen are temporal; but the things which are not seen are eternal" (2 Corinthians 4:18).

God has said He gave us also creative power to create in the power of our tongue. There is a battle/war going on now in the invisible world, which affects the visible world, and we cannot fight this battle with the weapons of the visible world, which we live in because they hold no power against the invisible world. For it is by the Spirit of

God (His power and His Word), which is through Jesus Christ our Lord, that overcomes the world—world meaning things that pertain to the visible world (material things and including the evil that dwells in it).

We have two enemies; the first one who exists in the unseen world is the devil. "Be sober, be vigilant; because your adversary the devil, as a roaring lion, walketh about, seeking whom he may devour" (1 Peter 5:8). The second one is within you, which is the carnal-minded man (your natural body) that follows after the things which are worldly (not of God). This enemy is self-pleasing/self-righteous. "But the natural man receiveth not the things of the Spirit of God: for they are foolishness unto him: neither can he know them, because they are spiritually discerned" (1 Corinthians 2:14).

> For they that are after the flesh do mind the things of the flesh; but they that are after the Spirit the things of the Spirit. For to be carnally minded is death; but to be spiritually minded is life and peace. Because the carnal mind is enmity against God: for it is not subject to the law of God, neither indeed can be. So then they that are in the flesh cannot please God. But ye are not in the

flesh, but the Spirit, if so be that the Spirit of God dwell in you. Now if any man have not the Spirit of Christ, he is none of his. And if Christ be in you, the body is dead because of sin; but the Spirit is life because of righteousness.

Romans 8:5–10

We are not equipped to fight and win over these two enemies alone! We cannot fight and win over these two enemies with an army! The visible world cannot overpower the invisible world, except God be with us! God says, "My little children, the battle is not yours; it belongs to God. You can only fight and win this war with the whole armor of God." The whole armor of God is what we need against these two enemies.

Where Is the Whole Armor of God Found, and How Do We Use this Armor?

The whole armor of God is found in the Word of God, which is in the Holy Bible (Ephesians 6:10–18). We use the whole armor of God to fight the unseen enemy, the devil. We must speak it by the power of our tongue and believe, imagining ourselves putting on God's armor. We must trust in God's Word because this is from God, and it is for us to stand against the devil and win. "What shall we then say to these things? If God be for us, who can be against us" (Romans 8:31)? We can imagine ourselves putting the whole armor of God on. The whole armor of God consists of eight principles, says the Holy Spirit of God.

What Are the Eight Principles?

> Finally, my brethren, be strong in the Lord, and in the power of his might. Put on the whole armour of God, that ye may be able to stand against the wiles of the devil. For we wrestle not against flesh and blood, but against principalities, against powers, against the rulers of the darkness of this world, against spiritual wickedness in high places. Wherefore take unto you the whole armour of God, that ye may be able to withstand in the evil day, and having done all, to stand. Stand therefore, having your loins girt about with truth, and having on the breastplate of righteousness, and your feet shod with the preparation of the gospel of peace; above all, taking the shield of faith, wherewith ye shall be able to quench all the fiery darts of the wicked. And take the helmet of salvation, and the sword of the

Spirit, which is the word of God: praying
always with all prayer and supplication in
the Spirit, and watching thereunto with all
perseverance and supplication for all saints.

Ephesians 6:10–18

We put on the whole armor of God by faith, believing
and declaring the truth of the Word of God, "We walk by
faith and not by sight" because the war against us is spiritual—it can only be fought spiritually in faith.

The Holy Spirit says, Let's point out the eight principles and what they mean. The eight principles are weapons that are spiritual. "For the weapons of our warfare are
not carnal, but mighty through God to the pulling down of
strongholds" (2 Corinthians 10:4).

The Eight Principles/Weapons We Are to Use Are:
- *Loins Girt*: "having loins girt about with truth"
  (Ephesians 6:14), we know that truth is the Word of
  God, which anchors you. "Sanctify them through
  thy truth: thy word is truth" (John 17:17).

- *Breastplate*: "the breastplate of righteousness"
  (Ephesians 6:14) protects our heart because it is
  the righteousness of Christ that defends us. "Being

filled with the fruits of righteousness, which are by Jesus Christ, unto the glory and praise of God" (Philippians 1:11).

- *Feet Shod*: "your feet shod with the preparation of the gospel of peace" (Ephesians 6:14), the peace that comes from God, which allows us to stand in the assurance, with God. "He brought me up also out of a horrible pit, out of the miry clay, and set my feet upon a rock, and established my goings" (Psalm 40:2).

- *Shield of Faith*: "taking the shield of faith" (Ephesians 6:15); by trusting in God/His Word, we are able to stop the evil that comes against us.

- *Helmet of Salvation*: "take the helmet of salvation" (Ephesians 6:17), we must ask God to have the mind of Christ, "Let this mind be in you, which was also in Christ Jesus" (Philippians 2:5).

- *Sword of the Spirit*: "the sword of the spirit, which is the Word of God" (Ephesians 6:17). "For the word of God is quick, and powerful, and sharper than any two-edged sword, piercing even to the dividing asunder of soul and spirit, and of the joints and marrow, and is a discerner of the thoughts and intents of the heart" (Hebrews 4:12).

- *Praying Always*: "praying always with all prayer and supplication in the spirit" (Ephesians 6:18), "Pray without ceasing" (1 Thessalonians 5:17). Praying calls God's attention toward us; we're asking for His help. "For with God, nothing shall be impossible" (Luke 1:37). "I can do all things through Christ which strengtheneth me" (Philippians 4:13).

- *Watching Thereunto*: "and watching thereunto with all perseverance" (Ephesians 6:18), watching/staying alert that we are not taken by surprise so that we are prepared. "Watch ye therefore, and pray always, that ye may be accounted worthy to escape all these things that shall come to pass, and to stand before the Son of man" (Luke 21:36). "Blessed are those servants, whom the Lord when he cometh shall find watching: verily I say unto you, that he shall gird himself, and make them to sit down to meat, and will come forth and serve them. And if he shall come in the second watch, or come in the third watch, and find them so, blessed are those servants" (Luke 12:37–38). The whole armor of God protects, sustains, equips, and prepares us to stand against our adversary, the devil.

How Do We Put On the Whole Armor of God?

We know that the Word of God is spirit and life. We also know that the Word of God is most powerful. God says, "It is the spirit that quickeneth; the flesh profiteth nothing: the words that I speak unto you, they are spirit, and they are life" (John 6:63). Again, we put on the whole armor of God by faith and with the power of our tongue. "Death and life are in the power of the tongue: and they that love it shall eat the fruit thereof" (Proverbs 18:21).

The enemy is in the spirit realm, but he affects the physical realm where we are through the minds of the people; therefore, in our fight against him, we need God/His Word, who is Spirit and the only weapon able to conquer him. By renewing our spiritual mind, which is also our heart, with the Word of God, placing God's Word on our heart, we will then see from our heart that our tongue shall speak. "Keep thy heart with all diligence; for out of it are the issues of life" (Proverbs 4:23). Therefore by speaking and having faith, we activate the power God has given us through His Holy Spirit. For if we think we can by the Word of God, then we can if our heart trusts in God. "For as he thinketh in his heart, so is he: Eat and drink, saith he to thee; but his heart is not with thee" (Proverbs 23:7). "Therefore I say unto you, What things soever ye desire, when we pray, believe that ye receive them, and ye shall have them" (Mark 11:24). "Nay, in all these things we are more than conquerors through him that loved us" (Romans 8:37). "Thou therefore, my son, be strong in the grace that is in Christ Jesus. And the things that thou hast heard of me among many witnesses, the same commit thou to faithful men, who shall be able to teach others also" (2 Timothy 2:1–2). The Word of God is vital to our existence; again, I will say because the Word is God with us (Emmanuel). God reminds us, "Do not fear." Fear blocks God from helping us. God is for us, do not be afraid because no one and nothing is greater than God. Amen.

God said, "Because he hath set his love upon me, therefore will I deliver him: I will set him on high because he hath known my name" (Psalm 91:14).

I love the Lord because he hath heard my voice and my supplications. Because he hath inclined his ear unto me, therefore will I call upon him as long as I live. The sorrows of death compassed me, and the pain of hell gat hold upon me: I found trouble and sorrow. Then called I upon the name of the Lord; O Lord I beseech thee, deliver my soul. Gracious is the Lord, and righteous; yea, our God is merciful. The Lord preserveth the simple: I was brought low, and he helped me. Return unto thy rest, O my soul; for the Lord hath dealt bountifully with thee. For thou hast delivered my soul from death, mines eyes from tears, and my feet from falling. I will walk before the Lord in the land of the living.

Psalm 116:1–9

Amen.

Golden Nuggets

"And from the days of John the Baptist until now the kingdom of heaven suffereth violence, and the violent take it by force" (Matthew 11:12).

• What Does This Mean?

There are those who are violently taken heaven by force; for example, John the Baptist, though he walked the earth, was in the kingdom of heaven, was taken and violently killed. Even though Jesus was willing to die on the cross for mankind, He was taken and violently killed also. The believers of Jesus Christ that do the will of God are also under attack. This violent attack is governed by Satan (the devil). This is why we need to put on the whole armor of God. Amen.

• What Is the Kingdom of Heaven?

The kingdom of heaven is where God (Jesus) rules and makes Himself known; the kingdom of heaven is spiritual, and you can only enter it through Jesus. The believers of Jesus Christ are in the kingdom of heaven. This means that God is with all who believe. Jesus brought His kingdom to the believers. As the Scriptures are accurate, in the kingdom of heaven, the believers, followers of Jesus, who suffereth violence, are under attack, and the violent take it by force. The unbelievers are deliberately interrupting God's will with all manner of ungodliness. "For the wrath of God is revealed from heaven against all ungodliness and unrighteousness of men, who hold the truth in un-righteousness" (Romans 1:18). "Dearly beloved, avenge not yourselves, but rather give place unto wrath: for it is written, Vengeance is mine; I will repay, saith the Lord" (Romans 12:19).

God says, use the weapons of God from God, again,

> Pray without ceasing. In every thing give thanks: for this is the will of God in Christ Jesus concerning you. Quench not the Spir-it. Despise not prophesyings. Prove all things; hold fast that which is good. Ab-stain from all appearance of evil. And the very God of peace sanctify you wholly, and I pray God your whole spirit and soul and body be preserved blameless unto the com-ing of our Lord Jesus Christ. Faithful is he that calleth you, who also will do it. Breth-ren, pray for us. Greet all the brethren with an holy kiss. I charge you by the Lord that this epistle be read unto all the holy breth-ren. The grace of our Lord Jesus Christ be with you. Amen.

1 Thessalonians 5:17–28

"For the weapons of our warfare are not carnal, but mighty through God to the pulling down of strongholds" (2 Corinthians 10:4). "Put on the whole armour of God, that ye may be able to stand against the wiles of the devil" (Ephesians 6:11). In order to fight the enemy and win as Jesus did, we must be in Christ, accept Jesus as our Lord and Savior, because we are strong in Him, then we can do what He did—declare that "*It is written*"! "And Jesus answered and said unto him, Get thee behind me, Satan: for it is written, Thou shall worship the Lord thy God, and him only shalt thou serve" (Luke 4:8). Amen.

"Two Kinds of People"

"For the wrath of God is revealed from heaven against all ungodliness and unrighteousness of men, who hold the truth in unrighteousness" (Romans 1:18).

"He that followeth after righteousness and mercy findeth life, righteousness, and honour" (Proverbs 21:21).

I Pray!

I thank You, dear Lord, for my help comes from You. Oh, Lord, for You have made heaven and earth, You have watched over my loved ones and me faithfully, in You will I trust. When I am forsaken by others, You continue to allow me to lay down and sleep in both peace and safety, "How precious also are thy thoughts unto me, O God! How great is the sum of them! If I should count them, they are more in number than the sand: when I awake, I am still with thee" (Psalm 139:17–18). I will praise You because You shall preserve my soul from evil, and You will keep me from hell, in Jesus' name. Amen.

Chapter 10

The Spirit of Truth & Discernment

In knowing and believing God's Word, "What shall we then say to these things? If God be for us, who can be against us" (Romans 8:31)? Jesus says, "I am the vine, ye are the branches: He that abideth in me, and I in him, the same bringeth forth much fruit: for without me ye can do nothing" (John 15:5). "My people are destroyed for lack of knowledge: because thou hast rejected knowledge, I will also reject thee, that thou shalt be no priest to me: seeing thou has forgotten the law of thy God, I will also forget thy children" (Hosea 4:6).

"Howbeit when he, the Spirit of truth, is come, he will guide you into all truth: for he shall not speak of himself; but whatsoever he shall hear, that shall he speak: and he will shew you things to come" (John 16:13). Amen.

Who Is the Spirit of Truth?

"Even the Spirit of truth; whom the world cannot receive, because it seeth him not, neither knoweth him: but ye know him; for He dwelleth with you, and shall be in you" (John 14:17). The Spirit of truth is the Holy Spirit of God in us. He always speaks the truth to the believers, which He hears. We will explore together who the Holy Spirit is in the upcoming chapters, as I am instructed by God.

We Must not Grieve the Holy Spirit: What Does This Mean?

To grieve the Holy Spirit is when you do not obey God. He said we must meditate on the Word of God. When you do not renew your mind daily with the Word, when your heart is far from God, when your tongue speaks corrupt words, when you lie, this grieves the Holy Spirit. Lying is a language, and this language is not from God. To those who learn or practice this language of lying, God is not your Father, the one who speaks this language is of the devil, he persuades you to lie; know this, "Ye are of your father the devil, and the lusts of your father ye will do. He was a murderer from the beginning, and abode not in the truth, because there is no truth in him. When he speaketh a lie, he speaketh of his own: for he is a liar and the father of it" (John 8:44). God says, "Wherefore putting away lying, speak every man truth with his neighbor: for we are members one of another" (Ephesians 4:25). Jesus says, "But he spake of the temple of his body" (John 2:21).

"God is not a man, that he should lie; neither the son of man, that he should repent: hath he said, and shall he not do it" (Numbers 23:19)? When you worry and do not trust God, when you do not forgive, when you are angry and sin, when you do anything that is against God's will, when you choose not to love, and when you do not pray, the Holy Spirit is grieved, suffering the loss of you. "And grieve not the Holy Spirit of God, whereby ye are sealed unto the day of redemption" (Ephesians 4:30).

If the Comforter/Holy Spirit is in you, and you do not grieve Him, He will tell you which voice is true. For example, if you hear your mom's or your dad's voice out of a small group of people talking to you, wouldn't you recognize it? The Holy Spirit keeps you steady on the right path because He knows all things that pertain to God. You are a dear friend to Him; He knows that friends are a blessing from God, and as your friend, He will always guide us in the way we must go; He has our best interest at heart. "Henceforth I call you not servants; for the servant knoweth not what his lord doeth: but I have called you friends; for all things that I have heard of my Father I have made known unto you" (John 15:15). "Be ye angry, and sin not: let not the sun go down upon your wrath" (Ephesians 4:26). "Let no corrupt communication proceed out of your mouth, but that which is good to the use of edifying, that it may minister grace unto the hearers" (Ephesians 4:29). The Holy Spirit says, "If you get angry, do not sin/do wrong things, least this is how the devil gains immediate access into your life and causes havoc!" "A soft answer turneth away wrath: but grievous words stir up anger" (Proverbs 15:1). "Whoso keepeth his mouth and his tongue keepeth his soul from troubles" (Proverbs 21:23). "My sheep hear my voice, and I know them, and they follow me: and I give unto them eternal life; and they shall never perish, neither shall any man pluck them out of my hand" (John 10:27–28). "God is a Spirit: and they that worship him must worship him in spirit and in truth" (John 4:24). "This I say then, Walk in the Spirit, and ye shall not fulfill the lust of the flesh. For the flesh lusteth against the Spirit, and the Spirit against the flesh: and these are contrary the one to the other: so that ye cannot do the things that ye would" (Galatians 5:16–17). "But the natural man receiveth not the things of the Spirit of God: for they are foolishness unto him: neither can he know them, because they are spiritually discerned" (1 Corinthians 2:14). We must walk in the Spirit in order to have discernment.

What Does Discernment Mean?

The Google Dictionary on the Internet says discernment means *"the ability to judge well."* The Holy Spirit says it is being able to make the right decisions according to God's Word/will.

What Does "To Walk in the Spirit" Mean?

The Holy Spirit of God says to walk in the Spirit means to walk with God and to do the things that pertain to God, to do His will. To walk in the Spirit, we must continuously meditate on the Word of God both day and night, to be careful to do what God asks, and we must pray. When we obey the Word of God, this trains us to hear and understand His Word; we are also able to receive clear instructions from the Holy Spirit, who dwells in us because we are feeding our spirit man/inner man, strengthening Him. By doing these things and having faith in God, we build a relationship with God and are able to recognize the voice of God. For some, God gives us the right to have the mind of Christ, to know the things of God. We who walk with God shall be prophets of God, able to teach the gospel of Jesus Christ, says the Holy Spirit.

"Then shall we know, if we follow on to know the Lord: his going forth is prepared as the morning; and he shall come unto us as the rain, as the latter and former rain unto the earth" (Hosea 6:3). "Neither say they in their heart, Let us now fear the Lord our God, that giveth rain, both the former and the latter, in his season: he reserveth unto us the appointed weeks of the harvest" (Jeremiah 5:24).

I understand what was stated above as the Holy Spirit speaks—in the days to come, God will give the believers a fresh outpouring of His Spirit, that we may be prepared to win souls for Jesus Christ, amen. I know all these things that I speak/write to be true, and they are from God. How do I know? I know because my natural self is not able to understand the things of God by itself; therefore, it has to be the Holy Spirit that speaks through me, along with studying/hearing the Word of God continuously throughout the day. Renewing my spirit makes me able to identify with the Word of God and the things that pertain to God. I see that the Word of God does what it says it does; it strengthens our spirit man to relate to God in His environment, that we may know the glorious and deep things of God.

"But there is a God in heaven that revealeth secrets, and maketh known to the king Nebuchadnezzar what shall be in the latter days. Thy dream, and the visions of thy head upon thy bed, are these" (Daniel 2:28). "Surely the Lord God will do nothing, but he revealeth his secret unto his servants the prophets" (Amos 3:7). "The secret things belong unto the Lord our God: but those things which are revealed belong unto us and to our children forever that we may do all the words of this law" (Deuteronomy 29:29). "For as he thinketh in his heart, so is he: Eat and drink, saith he to thee; but his heart is not with thee" (Proverbs 23:7). "But the end of all things is at hand: be ye therefore sober, and watch unto prayer" (1 Peter 4:7). "So teach us to number our days, that we may apply our hearts unto wisdom" (Psalm 90:12).

Let us pray. Father, help us to declare each day to be for Your glory. Amen. "The Father loveth the Son, and hath given all things into his hand" (John 3:35). "Let this mind be in you, which was also in Christ Jesus" (Philippians 2:5). "In this was manifested the love of God toward us, because that God sent his only begotten Son into the world, that we might live through him. Herein is love, not that we loved God, but that he loved us, and sent his Son to be the propitiation for our sins" (1 John 4:9–10). God in heaven is our Father, and He wants us to know His love towards what He has created (mankind), for we are not orphans, says the Holy Spirit. God says in His Word that He is our Father, "After this manner, therefore, pray ye: Our Father which art in heaven, Hallowed be thy name" (Matthew 6:9). "For ye are all the children of God by faith in Christ Jesus" (Galatians 3:26).

Golden Nugget

- We may know something like a Word or scripture, and every time we see it or hear it, we say to ourselves, *I know that, but it has not happened to me.* God says, You may know of something when you see it or when you hear it, but you will never have it; it will never work for you—until it reveals itself to you. In other words, you may know of something, but do you understand it really? And do you understand how it works? Behind every scripture/ every Word of God, there is God's Spirit. Also, if you do not have the indwelling of the Spirit of God, then how would you truly understand/have what's in the Scriptures/the Word of God?

Chapter 11

What Is Love?

For What Is Love?

The Holy Spirit of God instructs me that love is many things: Love is kind; love is patient; love is selfless; love is astonishing; love is sacrificial; love is giving; love is compassionate; love is merciful; love is nurturing; love shields; love encourages; love comforts; love defends; love soothes; love is extraordinary; love is good; love is personal; love is powerful; love is awesome; love edifies; love uplifts; love heals; love teaches; love is enjoyable; love is fulfilling; love is cleansing; love is joyful; love is satisfying; love is amusing; love is gentle; love is wise; love is freeing; love tolerates; love is empathetic; love is supportive; love is sympathetic; love is amazing; love is the most powerful strength there is. Experiencing the effects of love, know there is nothing that can compare to love or measure up to love; love is admirable; love is revolutionary; love is endless; love is a revelation to me; the only way to know, understand love and to truly have it or experience it immensely we must know the origin of love. Love is multifaceted, full of amazement, truth, and joy. Love is supernaturally wonderful. The majesty of love cannot be compared. Love is not a what but a who. Love is who God is. God is love.

Would You Like to Be Loved? Do You Need True Love?
Do You Want This Kind of Love or to Know True Love?

Do you want to receive and be able to give love? We all benefit tremendously by seeking after love (who is God) because even if you do not want love, you need love. Amen. Love is worth everything, meaning love is worth going after/seeking after; love is worth having now, and love will be worth having in eternity. Amen.

"And we have known and believed the love that God hath to us. God is love; and he that dwelleth in love dwelleth in God, and God in him" (1 John 4:16). "He that loveth not knoweth not God; for God is love" (1 John 4:8). Amen.

Golden Nuggets

- We learn from the Scriptures to love others as we love ourselves, but we must not become attached/ worship them because if we love another or love a particular thing more than God, it is called idol worship, and if we lose it, then it may make us feel like we want to die or we might become lost and grieve excessively.

- Be kind to one another because nothing is what it seems. Someone may look happy and put together, but in reality, they could be carrying a burden that is too much to bear. It is, therefore, good to be kind to one another always; who knows but God, you just might be the one that makes all the difference in their day. Amen.

- If you can be anything, be the change you want to see.

"Grace"

Humans are incredibly blessed because, by God's grace, we can share our righteousness: we get to laugh, cry, love, and live to see another day together. Amen.

Chapter 12

The Extent of God's Love

If only mankind knew the seriousness of walking away from God. When you turn from God, you, without knowing, turn towards the things that God would have never allowed you to see. Mankind would not have ever known death, the grave, sin, sickness, and evil of all kinds, only God, His love, His grace, and His mercy for mankind He commanded toward us. Now the questions are, How can God love us so? "What is man, that thou art mindful of him? and the son of man, that thou visitest him" (Psalm 8:4)? "And God said, Let us make man in our image, after our likeness: and let them have dominion over the fish of the sea, and over the fowl of the air, and over the cattle, and over all the earth, and over every creeping thing that creepeth upon the earth" (Genesis 1:26). If only mankind could really understand the extent of God's love toward us. God does not want us to die. He wants us to live; He has great plans for us. "Behold, what manner of love the Father hath bestowed upon us, that we should be called the sons of God: therefore, the world knoweth us not, because it knew him not" (1 John 3:1). "For God so loved the world, that he gave his only begotten Son, that whosoever believeth in him should not perish, but have everlasting life" (John 3:16). "But God commendeth his love toward us, in that, while we were yet sinners, Christ died for us" (Romans 5:8). "Whosoever believeth that Jesus is the Christ is born of God: and every one that loveth him that begat loveth him also that is begotten of him" (1 John 5:1).

I pray. Father, thank You for your love, may You please keep me humble, that I might always be able to live in the truth of Your love and be able to share with others, as You will it, in Jesus' name, amen. "Herein is love, not that we loved God, but that he loved us, and sent his Son to be the propitiation for our sins" (1 John 4:10).

I Pray

I pray, dear Lord, deliver me from the power of sin. Deliver me from the power of bondage. Deliver me from all illness and disease. Deliver me from limited resources. Supply all my needs and deliver me from evil. Oh God/Father in heaven, restore in me Your joy and allow me to remain in Your presence, that I may be free to serve You always, in Jesus' name. Amen.

As I heard the Lord respond, "Fear thou not; for I am with thee: be not dismayed; for I am thy God: I will strengthen thee; yea, I will help thee; yea, I will uphold thee with the right hand of my righteousness" (Isaiah 41:10). Amen.

Golden Nugget

- The promises of God are complete; we might as well grab hold of as many as possible and believe while we are able to. Amen. "For all the promises of God in him are yea, and in him Amen, unto the glory of God by us. Now he which stablisheth us with you in Christ, and hath anointed us, is God; who hath also sealed us, and given the earnest of the Spirit in our hearts" (2 Corinthians 1:20–22).

Chapter 13

A Father's Love

A Father's unparalleled love for His children is undeniable. It's a love so true it's not understandable—a Father willing to allow a great part of Himself to die in order for His children to live. A Father's love—how much did He give so that His children might live and live more abundantly? A Father's love that defies all logic. A Father's love reveals His heart for His children. A Father's love stands the test of time. His love, so pure and powerful, saves, and His love saves for eternity all His children that love Him. What manner of love is this? A Father's love that is unmeasured, unwavering, unchallenged, unconditional, unfailing, and unprecedented toward His children. This is the agape love, the highest kind of love one could not even dream of or fathom (a Father's love); this is in reference to God's love towards us, who is our Father in heaven. "For God so loved the world, that he gave his only begotten Son, that whosoever believeth in him should not perish, but have everlasting life. For God sent not his Son into the world to condemn the world; but that the world through him might be saved" (John 3:16, 17). "For I am persuaded, that neither death, nor life, nor angels, nor principalities, nor powers, nor things present, nor things to come, nor height, nor depth, nor any other creature, shall be able to separate us from the love of God, which is in Christ Jesus our Lord" (Romans 8:38, 39). "That Christ may dwell in your hearts by faith; that ye, being rooted and grounded in love, may be able to comprehend with all saints what is the breadth, and length, and depth, and height; and to know the love of Christ, which passeth knowledge, that ye might be filled with all the fulness of God" (Ephesians 3:17–19).

Behold, what manner of love the Father hath bestowed upon us, that we should be called the sons of God: therefore the world knoweth us not, because it knew him not. Beloved, now are we the sons of God, and it doth not yet appear what we shall be: but we know that, when he shall appear, we shall be like him; for we shall see him as he is. And every man that hath this hope in him purifieth himself, even as he is pure.

1 John 3:1–3

The law of the Lord is perfect, converting the soul: the testimony of the Lord is sure, making wise the simple. The statues of the Lord are right, rejoicing the heart: the commandment of the Lord is pure, enlightening the eyes. The fear of the Lord is clean, enduring forever. The judgments of the Lord are true and righteous altogether. More to be desired are they than gold, yea, than much fine gold: sweeter also than honey and the honeycomb. Moreover, by them is thy servant warned: and in keeping of them there is great reward.

Psalm 19:7–11

God says, "Remember the former things of old: for I am God, and there is none else; I am God, and there is none like me" (Isaiah 46:9). "But he answered and said, It is written, Man shall not live by bread alone, but by every word that proceedeth out of the mouth of God" (Matthew 4:4). "Every word of God is pure: he is a shield unto them that put their trust in him" (Proverbs 30:5). "But he said, Yea rather, blessed are they that hear the word of God, and keep it" (Luke 11:28). Father, "Sanctify them through thy truth: thy word is truth" (John 17:17). "This book of the law shall not depart out of thy mouth; but thou shalt meditate therein day and night, that thou mayest observe to do according to all that is written therein: for then thou shalt make thy way prosperous, and then thou shalt have good success" (Joshua 1:8). "And be not conformed to this world: but be ye transformed by the renewing of your mind, that ye may prove what is that good, and acceptable, and perfect, will of God" (Romans 12:2). And "Pray without ceasing" (1 Thessalonians 5:17). Amen.

How Do We Renew Our Mind, and What Does This Mean?

To renew is to restore, strengthen, revive, or feed our spiritual minds. We renew our minds by studying and hearing the Word of God. If we do not renew or feed our spiritual minds, what will happen? The revelation of the Holy Spirit of God says our spiritual minds are starving! What happens to something when it does not receive the thing it needs to sustain itself? It dies slowly, but first, depression creeps in. One part of our mind thinks separate from our body yet lives inside our body. Our mind must be fed in three parts: physical, spiritual, and through our senses; all equally important; the food that enters through your physical mouth, the spiritual food "relating to or affecting the human spirit or soul." For example, the things you cannot see but are vital like what the Word of God does and the food that enters through our four other senses: sight, smell, hearing, and touch. God then says knowledge is food also. "My people are destroyed for lack of knowledge: because thou hast rejected knowledge, I will also reject thee, that thou shalt be no priest to me: seeing thou hast forgotten the law of thy God, I will also forget thy children" (Hosea 4:6). Our mind is very powerful; it has the ability to do things we cannot even imagine. It constantly works, whether you know it or not, and it uses a lot of fuel, so it can become exhausted quickly.

Why Does God Say We Must Renew Our Minds with His Word?

We must renew our minds with God's Word so that other things will not enter us and take residence. Know this, whatever is on our mind tends to dominate our being, and we will move in the direction of the state of our mind. Renewing our minds is the will of God, which is for our benefit. Amen.

The Lord God says, What and how are you supplying what your mind needs to operate at its best, and do you know what your mind needs? Our mind/whole body must have the proper nourishment; we have a physical mind relating to our fleshly body, and we have a spiritual mind which relates to our spiritual body.

The Spirit Man that Lives in Us, What Is He?

The Holy Spirit teaches me that our spirit man is our spiritual body, which cannot be seen with our physical eyes, and our spiritual body connects us to the spiritual realm that does exist. Our spirit man communicates with God (connects us to God), and our soul is the mediator between our spirit man and our physical body. For example, our soul is our character, personality, feelings, reasoning, will, and mind. I believe the soul has an influence on the spirit man and our physical body; the spirit man is also called the inward man, receiving from both our soul and the unseen world; as the inward man receives from our soul, which connects to our physical body (everything that pertains to the world), the unseen world that connects us to God. I, therefore, believe our physical body, which receives from our soul, carries out or expresses the things related to our soul and spirit. Our spiritual body, together with our soul, is located in the core of our physical heart since our soul contains our mind and all the other characteristics located in our heart.

I also believe this is why God says to guard our hearts because everything that is important comes from it. God's Word tells us to "Keep thy heart with all diligence; for out of it are the issues of life" (Proverbs 4:23). "A good man out of the good treasure of his heart bringeth forth that which is good; and an evil man out of the evil treasure of his heart bringeth forth that which is evil: for of the abundance of the heart his mouth speaketh" (Luke 6:45). "The heart is deceitful above all things, and desperately wicked: who can know it? I the Lord search the heart, I try the reins, even to give every man according to his ways, and according to the fruit of his doings" (Jeremiah 17:9–10). "Grant thee according to thine heart and fulfil all thy counsel" (Psalm 20:4). "And ye shall seek me and find me when ye shall search for me with all your heart" (Jeremiah 29:13). "Blessed are they that keep his testimonies, and that seek him with the whole heart" (Psalm 119:2). "He hath made everything beautiful in his time: also he hath set the world in their heart, so that no man can find out the work that God maketh from the beginning to the end" (Ecclesiastes 3:11).

I understand the above scripture to mean this: at the time God made everything, He made it all beautiful. In our/mankind's heart, God placed the appearance of the world, that in order for us to fully understand its beginning to end, "we must turn back to Him." Amen. "But the Lord said unto Samuel, Look not on his countenance, or on the height of his stature; because I have refused him: for the Lord seeth not a man seeth; for man looketh on the outward appearance, but the Lord looketh on the heart" (1

Samuel 16:7). "Let not thine heart decline to her ways, go not astray in her paths" (Proverbs 7:25). "Trust in the Lord with all thine heart; and lean not unto thine own understanding. In all thy ways acknowledge him, and he shall direct thy paths" (Proverbs 3:5–6). God says to have no fear; He is with us. We must intentionally keep our hearts from evil and seek the Lord that we may be restored, and in our quiet time while reading, we will feel the presence of God, says the Holy Spirit.

Let us pray, "Create in me a clean heart, O God; and renew a right spirit within me" (Psalm 51:10). "I sought the Lord, and he heard me, and delivered me from all my fears" (Psalm 34:4). I, therefore, believe amongst the many scriptures of the Word of God, God refers to all matters from out of our hearts. Please be advised this is what I believe through the Holy Spirit. Again, I say that our spiritual mind, which is within our spirit man, located in our heart, is the thinking or reasoning or receiving part expressed by our soul, whereby the physical brain itself receives messages from our soul and the environment, using our five senses in response, sending the messages throughout all parts of the body. The physical brain/carnal mind and our spinal cord together are the command center, constantly sending messages and receiving messages throughout our physical body, as I remember. I also believe our physical brain is limited for now, and part of it is a house in which all our memories are kept even before birth.

To me, our physical mind, or a large part of it, is asleep and is like a storage unit containing knowledge that one day when we are face to face with God, we will have use of our whole mind (be completely woke). Our spiritual body connects with our soul and God; our soul and physical body connect/communicate with each other. Again, our soul connects with both our spiritual body and our physical body, receiving from each one simultaneously. The Holy Spirit says our soul contains our will and can be overruled by our carnal mind and/or by our spiritual mind. Be it as it may, to me, since the inward man/the spirit man must be renewed daily, then our physical mind, which is called in the Bible our carnal mind, this area of our body, I believe, as stated above, is the storage area of the thoughts which originated from our soul, spirit, and environment can be fed the Word of God. These thoughts that came from out of the mind, located in the spirit man, are what I believe to be called our spiritual mind. The physical mind—this area known as our carnal mind—is subjected to the things of the flesh, our physical body (our five senses), and the things pertaining to the world.

To me, God addresses all the issues concerning life,

in aspect from the state of our heart (our spiritual mind) and not from our physical mind/carnal mind. The spiritual body and the physical body war against one another within you. Why is this? Because the physical body longs to self-gratify (being selfish), and the spiritual body seeks after the things of God. "For to be carnally minded is death, but to be spiritually minded is life and peace. Because the carnal mind is enmity against God: for it is not subject to the law of God, neither indeed can be. So, then they that are in the flesh cannot please God" (Romans 8:6–8). This is why God says, "O generation of vipers, how can ye, being evil, speak good things? For out of the abundance of the heart the mouth speaketh" (Matthew 12:34). In other words, the Holy Spirit explains that the physical mind/ carnal mind, since it pertains to things of the earth realm, longs for the things that are against God, which are evil. He also explains that words are so powerful they move the seat of our soul.

What Is the Seat of Our Soul?

I believe the seat of our soul is our heart. The Holy Spirit then says our heart is so important that God made our heart the first organ in the fetus of mankind to form, as I remember learning. Therefore, every issue that is in our life comes from the things in our heart; this is why God places emphasis on renewing our mind with His Word, because in renewing our mind, we strengthen both our spiritual mind and soul, which is in our heart, also strengthening our physical mind by the Word of God. Our spirit man connects with our soul—within him are the eyes, the ears, and the mind of our heart spiritually, which is located in the core of our physical heart, and he/our spirit man is who God communicates with. Amen.

Golden Nugget

- The Lord God says the spiritual mind of mankind located in our heart can connect with the things of God—it is the most incredible part of the body. Why? Because it has the ability to adapt, think, choose, and create. From out of the abundance of the heart, whatever our spiritual mind believes, our entire body and everything around us may follow. Amen.

Chapter 14

The Eyes of Your Heart

In the prayer at the beginning of this book, I mentioned "the eyes of your heart," what does this mean? I am referring to the eyes, the ears, and the mind of the inner man, who is the spirit man. Just as the Holy Spirit explains above, the spirit man, who is also the spiritual body, collaborates with the soul, located in the core of our physical heart, from out of your heart are the issues of life.

The spirit man within us is the inner man/inward man (our true self). God has allowed us to know, "And hath raised us up together, and made us sit together in heavenly places in Christ Jesus" (Ephesians 2:6). To raise us up to sit in heavenly places can only be with our spiritual body. "That he would grant you according to the riches of his glory, to be strengthened with might by his Spirit in the inner man" (Ephesians 3:16). "For which cause we faint not; but though our outward man perish, yet the inward man is renewed day by day" (2 Corinthians 4:16). By the Word of God. "Blessed be the God and Father of our Lord Jesus Christ, who hath blessed us with all spiritual blessings in heavenly places in Christ" (Ephesians 1:3).

God has blessed our spiritual bodies through Jesus Christ, our Lord. The spirit man cannot be fed the same food which our physical body eats for nourishment because natural food has no effect on the spiritual body. Although the spiritual body of a man, woman, and child do exist in us, the spirit man is separate, and his food is the Word of God; remember the Word was God, who is Spirit. God's Word is good for our spirit man because the Word supplies all the nourishment our spirit man needs to thrive. That is why God says, "Taste and see that the Lord is good" because God's Word is good food for our spirit body. We also know that faith is spiritual, to believe without seeing. Your whole body must have the proper nourishment, your physical body needs physical food, and your spiritual body needs spiritual food, which is the Word of God, in order to function at our original intent. We are made up of three parts: 1) our spiritual mind is in our spirit man/spiritual body, also known as the inward man; 2) our body is our physical body, also known as our flesh or carnal body, and; 3) our soul, which is our character/personality. We are three separate parts within a single body. We are the sum of our parts, equaling one individual. Whereby God Almighty is three of the same: God the Father, God the Son, and God the Holy Spirit. He's expressed/manifested Himself as three individuals, yet at the same time, they exist as One. Amen.

Golden Nugget

- What if the Father, the Word, and the Holy Ghost
  are like a symphony? What if mankind was the fi-
  nal part of the symphony? If this is true, then believers will be in harmony in the end, and man will
  be not equal to, but be in sync with, God. Amen.

Chapter 15

Food

Food is masterful; its purpose is to give, to give in a way you may or may not even know. Food does what it was created to do: feed our bodies and speak to our souls. We all know that the body must have it; we need food to grow, to stay alive, but what most do not know is God gave us food to do so much more. We all know food can taste oh so good; it can comfort you; it can help give you good health; it can make you feel happy. Food is a wonderful creation from God if you are able to eat it.

How Splendid Is Food, from the Garden or Farm to the Table?

Food can restore, unite, be therapeutic, be relational, or food can teach. Food is extraordinarily brilliant and should never be abused because when you consume it with wrong intentions, it can become fatal. For example, if you are eating wrongly and overeating continually. So, love food and keep it sensible, you will get much nourishment by having it. Learn to eat good food so that you can take care of yourself. This shows appreciation to God for creating you and so much more. What you may not know about food is it reminds us that we must meet our body's needs, which sustains us, not just physically but spiritually. Now, let's briefly talk about the two foods needed now, but later in the upcoming chapters, we will get more into it.

We have two bodies, a physical one and a spiritual one, and they both need food. We all know our physical body needs natural food, food pertaining to the earth realm. But the spiritual body, the one you are not able to see with your physical eye, needs food from God, which is written in the Holy Bible. "But he answered and said, It is written, Man shall not live by bread alone, but by every word that proceedeth out of the mouth of God" (Matthew 4:4). So we must feed our physical body natural food and our spiritual body the Word of God to be merry, meaning to have a joyous life. God said in His Word, "Jesus saith unto them, My meat is to do the will of him that sent me, and to finish his work" (John 4:34). God shows us how meat—which is also food—is His will, that we are to do as Jesus did. Every word that comes out of the mouth of God is delicious because the Word is good for the life of mankind. This is why God says, "O taste and see that the Lord is good: blessed is the man that trusteth in him" (Psalm 34:8). God speaks, "Heaven and earth shall pass away, but my words shall not pass away" (Matthew 24:35). "For it is so, My Word goes forth since the beginning of time, has always been and will always be indestructible," says the Holy Spirit of God.

Can Any Living Thing Live without Food?

Without food, that which is alive will surely die. Food is sacred, especially spiritual food, which is the Word of God because it connects us to God. "And as they were eating, Jesus took bread, and blessed it, and brake it, and gave it to the disciples and said, Take, eat; this is my body" (Matthew 26:26).

> Then Jesus said unto them, Verily, verily, I say unto you, Except ye eat the flesh of the Son of man, and drink his blood, ye have no life in you. Whoso eateth my flesh, and drinketh my blood, hath eternal life; and I will raise him up at the last day. For my flesh is meat indeed, and my blood is drink indeed. He that eateth my flesh, and drinketh my blood, dwelleth in me, and I in him.

John 6:53–56

Every word that proceedeth out of the mouth of God, again, is spiritual food, and when we choose to live by the

Word of God, it is meat and drink to establish and sustain our life. The Holy Spirit shows us how spiritual food is what Jesus was referring to, and it is symbolic of the life of Jesus on earth and His death on the cross. In remembrance of Jesus' life (the Word), His death, which paid the price for our sins, and His shed blood (to believe) are mankind's saving grace, which is everlasting. To those who live by the Word of God, we are, therefore, joint-heirs of Christ Jesus. Thank You, Lord, for both spiritual and natural food. We must remember to thank God for the food that we receive because when we thank Him, He blesses the food for our bodies. To give thanks to God is His will for us, and blessings from God are always for our benefit and good. Amen. Remember this, if anyone should hold something against someone, have strife or unforgiveness in their hearts, you must therefore repent of yourself and forgive others for their trespasses, or you will not be worthy to partake in the eating and drinking of the body of Christ Jesus. "If anyone partakes anyway, without true forgiveness in their heart, you will have put sickness upon your own bodies, due to your unforgiving heart," says the Holy Spirit of God.

God wants us to understand that if we do not truly repent and truly forgive, we are governed by another spirit that is unrighteous, which is not of God, and God forbids that spirit to be righteous. We must be obedient to God's

Word by doing what He tells us to do because God is the only One who will always be righteous in all things He says to do. Amen.

> For I have received of the Lord that which also I delivered unto you, that the Lord Jesus the same night in which he was betrayed took bread: and when he had given thanks, he brake it, and said, Take, eat: this is my body, which is broken for you: this do in remembrance of me. After the same manner also he took the cup, when he had supped, saying, This cup is the new testament in my blood: this do ye, as oft as ye drink it, in remembrance of me. For as often as ye eat this bread, and drink this cup, ye do shew the Lord's death till he comes. Wherefore whosoever shall eat this bread, and drink this cup of the Lord, unworthily, shall be guilty of the body and blood of the Lord. But let a man examine himself, and so let him eat of that bread, and drink of that cup. For he that eateth and drinketh unworthily, eateth and drinketh damnation to himself, not discerning the Lord's body. For this cause, many are weak and sickly among you and many sleep. For if we would judge ourselves, we should not be judged. But

when we are judged, we are chastened of the Lord, that we should not be condemned with the world.

1 Corinthians 11:23–32

This is the bread which cometh down from heaven, that a man may eat thereof, and not die. I am the living bread which came down from heaven: if any man eat of this bread, he shall live forever: and the bread that I will give is my flesh, which I will give for the life of the world. The Jews therefore strove among themselves, saying, how can this man give us his flesh to eat? Then Jesus said unto them, Verily, verily, I say unto you, Except ye eat the flesh of the Son of man, and drink his blood, ye have no life in you. Whoever eateth my flesh, and drinketh my blood, hath eternal life; and I will raise him up at the last day. For my flesh is meat indeed, and my blood is drink indeed. He that eateth my flesh, and drinketh my blood, dwelleth in me, and I in him. As the living Father hath sent me, and I live by the Father: so he that eateth me, even he shall live by me.

The Holy Spirit says, in "Eating my flesh and drinking my blood," do this in remembrance of Jesus. This means if we honor God and choose to follow Jesus, then the life of Jesus is in us.

What Is Eternal Life?

Some might answer this question like this: eternal life means living forever, but Jesus says in the Holy Bible,

> These words spake Jesus, and lifted up his eyes to heaven, and said, Father, the hour is come; glorify thy Son, that thy Son also may glorify thee: as thou hast given him power over all flesh, that he should give eternal life to as many as thou hast given him. And this is life eternal, that they might know thee the only true God, and Jesus Christ, whom thou hast sent.

John 17:1–3

Jesus Prayed

> I pray not for the world, but them which thou hast given me; for they are thine. And

all mine are thine, and thine are mine, and I am glorified in them. And now I am no more in the world, but these are in the world, and I come to thee. Holy Father, keep through thine own name those whom thou hast given me, that they may be one, as we are. While I was with them in the world, I kept them in thy name: those that thou gavest me I have kept, and none of them is lost, but the son of perdition; that the scripture might be fulfilled.

John 17:9–12

Amen.

Golden Nuggets

- Sometimes, I cry if someone mistreats me, but I do not cry because of the harm done to me; my tears are for them and for God to have mercy on that one who initiated harm towards me. Our tears are a blessing from God; they can pray for mercy, even if we choose not to speak. My tears have cried, "Lord have mercy on the one who intended harm towards me and have mercy on me to forgive them righteously." Amen.

- "And let us not be weary in well doing: for in due season we shall reap, if we faint not" (Galatians 6:9). Jesus prays to the Father on our behalf, "I pray not that thou shouldest take them out of the world, but that thou shouldest keep them from the evil" (John 17:15).

- Finish what you start, to completion, that you may obtain peace. If there is no peace, then there is no hope. Peace is not negotiable; we must have it! In other words, do not give up on doing right, and in all you do, do it peacefully. "For God is not the author of confusion, but of peace, as in all churches of the saints" (1 Corinthians 14:33). "Thou wilt keep him in perfect peace, whose mind is stayed on thee: because he trusteth in thee" (Isaiah 26:3). "Blessed are the peacemakers: for they shall be called the children of God" (Matthew 5:9). "Now the Lord of peace himself give you peace always by all means. The Lord be with you all" (2 Thessalonians 3:16). Amen.

Why Did Jesus Die on the Tree Cross?

I've heard several stories, but the one

I am instructed to write is, as, in the beginning,

Adam and Eve ate the fruit of the forbidden tree.

To get to the point, Jesus being put up on the tree cross

symbolizes the return to where sin began

on the forbidden tree.

Adam ate the forbidden fruit, and in the Holy Bible,

Jesus on the tree symbolizes that He is the fruit

that we may eat instead; Jesus is our spiritual food.

Amen.

Thus far, the Holy Spirit says Jesus gave His life

that we may become the righteousness

of God through Christ.

In other words, where sin started, Jesus (God)

returned and began salvation, that we can be

holy again and be with God.

In the Scriptures, Jesus cries out and says, "Father, it is

finished." Now, we have a choice not to sin.

Amen.

Chapter 16

Comfort Food

The Word of God became my food, and the more I study, the better it gets. Each Word of God satisfies the time that I am in. The Word of God is like comfort food; you can never get enough of it. Taste and see that the Word of God is good. "O taste and see that the Lord is good: blessed is the man that trusteth in him" (Psalm 34:8). The Holy Spirit of the Lord God also says that God's human creation is unmatched, and there is no other creature under the sun, in heaven or under the earth, that is able to possess legally two bodies simultaneously, a physical body to dwell in the earth kingdom and a spiritual body to dwell in eternity. God has given mankind access and power, authority in two places, and to possess two bodies, physical and spiritual, existing both in the same body at the same time, all because of Jesus Christ. We know that "God is a Spirit: and they that worship him must worship him in spirit and in truth" (John 4:24).

> The Spirit itself beareth witness with our spirit, that we are the children of God: and

if children, then heirs; heirs of God, and joint-heirs with Christ; if so be that we suffer with him, that we may also be glorified together. For I reckon that the sufferings of this present time are not worthy to be compared with the glory which shall be revealed in us.

Romans 8:16–18

We know that God is Spirit, and for those who believe in Jesus, He speaks to us through His Spirit.

But God hath revealed them unto us by his Spirit: for the Spirit searcheth all things, yea, the deep things of God. For what man knoweth the things of a man, save the spirit of man which is in him? Even so, the things of God knoweth no man, but the Spirit of God. Now we have received, not the spirit of the world, but the spirit which is of God; that we might know the things that are freely given to us of God. Which things also we speak, not in the words which man's wisdom teacheth, but which the Holy Ghost teacheth; comparing spiritual things with spiritual. But the natural man received not the things of the Spirit of God: for they are foolishness unto him: neither can he know them, because they are spiritually discerned. But he that is spiritual judgeth all things, yet he himself is judged of no man. For who hath known the mind of the Lord, that he may instruct him? But we have the mind of Christ.

1 Corinthians 2:10–16

"But the Comforter, which is the Holy Ghost, whom the Father will send in my name, he shall teach you all things, and bring all things to your remembrance, whatsoever I have said unto you" (John 14:26).

The Holy Spirit is sent to us to give us the truth; He feeds us spiritually, He gives us strength, and He gives us the power to be able to search the deep things of God. Know this, "When thou goest out to battle against thine enemies, and seest horses, and chariots, and a people more than thou, be not afraid of them: for the Lord, thy God, is with thee which brought thee up out of the land of Egypt" (Deuteronomy 20:1). "And grieve not the Holy Spirit of God, whereby ye are sealed unto the day of redemption" (Ephesians 4:30). "And be renewed in the spirit of your mind" (Ephesians 4:23). "Set your affection on things above, not on things on the earth" (Colossians 3:2). "Let the word of Christ dwell in you richly in all wisdom; teaching and admonishing one another in psalms and hymns and spiritual songs, singing with grace in your hearts to the Lord" (Colossians 3:16).

"Every word of God is pure: he is a shield unto them that put their trust in him" (Proverbs 30:5). Lord, please, "Sanctify them through thy truth: thy word is truth" (John 17:17). "All scripture is given by inspiration of God, and is profitable for doctrine, for reproof, for correction, for instruction in righteousness: that the man of God may be perfect, thoroughly furnished unto all good works" (2 Timothy 3:16–17). "For the word of God is quick, and powerful, and sharper than any two-edged sword, piercing even to the dividing asunder of soul and spirit, and of the joint and marrow, and is a discerner of the thoughts and intents of the heart" (Hebrews 4:12). In other words, the Word of God is so powerful it is able to do impossible things, reaching the very areas that cannot be seen, and His Word knows the true intent of your thoughts and of your heart.

God's Word cannot be stopped, nor can God be fooled! God cannot be reduced to fit in our imagination! For there is no one, by reasoning or by explaining, who can erase

God! God wants us to know these are the things that God cannot do! He cannot be silenced! Because you may not hear Him does not mean He is not speaking! He cannot do evil, or be evil, nor can He sin! He cannot lie! He cannot grow weary! He cannot be compartmentalized! He cannot be reduced! He cannot die! He cannot be ignored! You cannot explain God away. In other words, there is no proof that God does not exist; the only truth is that we see the evidence in the manifestation of God in His daily blessings throughout the earth. The manifestation of God's spoken Word in designing an earthly suit (the human body) clearly proves that the body is a temporary home for our soul, mind, spirit, and for the Holy Ghost, all which God has made for Himself. We exist because of God, "For of him, and through him, and to him, are all things: to whom be glory forever. Amen" (Romans 11:36).

As we read above, all things belong to God; He made us, we are His creation; He is above everything, and He is at liberty to do as He pleases, in His timing. God says,

> Woe unto him that striveth with his Maker!
> Let the potsherd strive with the potsherds
> of the earth. Shall the clay say to him that
> fashioneth it, What makest thou? or thy
> work, He hath no hands? Woe unto him that

139

saith unto his father, What begettest thou? or to the woman, what hast thou brought forth? Thus saith the Lord, the Holy One of Israel, and his Maker, Ask me of things to come concerning my sons and concerning the work of my hands command ye me. I have made the earth, and created man upon it: I, even my hands, have stretched out the heavens, and all their host have I commanded.

Isaiah 45:9–12

God is our refuge and strength, a very present help in trouble. Therefore, will not we fear, though the earth be removed, and though the mountains be carried into the midst of the sea; Though the waters thereof roar and be troubled, though the mountains shake with the swelling thereof. Selah. There is a river, the streams whereof shall make glad the city of God, the holy place of the tabernacles of the Most High.

Psalm 46:1–4

We need the Word of God to have the abundance of

life, "For in him we live, and move, and have our being; as certain also of your own poets have said, For we are also his offspring" (Acts 17:28).

Where Can You Find the Word of God, and What Is the Word of God?

The Word of God is found in the Holy Bible. "All scripture is given by inspiration of God, and is profitable for doctrine, for reproof, for correction, for instruction in righteousness: that the man of God may be perfect, thoroughly furnished unto all good works" (2 Timothy 3:16–17). The Word of God is, as it says, "In the beginning was the Word, and the Word was with God, and the Word was God. The same was in the beginning with God. All things were made by him; and without him was not anything made that was made. In him was life; and the life was the light of men" (John 1:1–4). To point out above ("the Word was God"), we see the Word is God.

Looking in the Bible about the announcement of the Son of God to Joseph, the soon-to-be husband of Mary,

> But while he thought on these things, behold, the angel of the Lord appeared unto him in a dream, saying, Joseph, thou son of David, fear not to take unto thee Mary thy

wife: for that which is conceived in her is of the Holy Ghost. And she shall bring forth a son, and thou shalt call his name Jesus: for he shall save his people from their sins. Now all this was done, that it might be fulfilled which was spoken of the Lord by the prophet, saying, Behold, a virgin shall be with child, and shall bring forth a son, and they shall call his name Emmanuel, which being interpreted is, God with us.

Matthew 1:20–23

"And the Word was made flesh, and dwelt among us, (and we beheld his glory, the glory as of the only begotten of the Father,) full of grace and truth" (John 1:14). "For God so loved the world, that he gave his only begotten Son, that whosoever believeth in him should not perish, but have everlasting life" (John 3:16). "And lo a voice from heaven, saying, This is my beloved Son, in whom I am well pleased" (Matthew 3:17). "Jesus knowing that the Father had given all things into his hands and that he was come from God, and went to God" (John 13:3). "For in him dwelleth all the fulness of the Godhead bodily. And ye are complete in him, which is the head of all principality and power" (Colossians 2:9–10).

Who, being in the form of God, thought it not robbery to be equal with God: but made himself of no reputation, and took upon him the form of a servant, and was made in the likeness of men: and being found in fashion as a man, he humbled himself, and became obedient unto death, even the death of the cross. Wherefore God also hath highly exalted him, and given him a name which is above every name: that at the name of Jesus every knee should bow, of things in heaven, and things in earth, and things under the earth; and that every tongue should confess that Jesus Christ is Lord, to the glory of God the Father.

Philippians 2:6–11

God says Jesus is indispensable, "And Jesus came and spake unto them, saying, All power is given unto me in heaven and in earth" (Matthew 28:18). "Then spake Jesus again unto them, saying, I am the light of the world: he that followeth me shall not walk in darkness, but shall have the light of life" (John 8:12). "Jesus saith unto him, I am the way, the truth, and the life: no man cometh unto the Father, but by me" (John 14:6).

Why Is the Word of God So Important?

The Word of God is so important because the Word is God; He is in His Word. God's Word carries all authority; therefore, God says, "Live by Me." God makes Himself known to man through His Word. "In the beginning was the Word, and the Word was with God, and the Word was God" (John 1:1). "And the Word was made flesh, and dwelt among us, (and we beheld his glory, the glory as of the only begotten of the Father,) full of grace and truth" (John 1:14).

> That which was from the beginning, which we have heard, which we have seen with our eyes, which we have looked upon, and our hands have handled, of the Word of life; (For the life was manifested, and we have seen it, and bear witness, and shew unto you that eternal life, which was with the Father, and was manifested unto us;) that which we have seen and heard declare we unto you, that ye also may have fellowship with us: and truly our fellowship is with the Father, and with his Son Jesus Christ.
>
> **1 John 1:1–3**

Amen.

Can Anyone Understand the Word of God?

Yes, if we ask God for understanding through the Holy Spirit of God, God will open our spiritual eyes and ears to give us understanding to the truth of His Word; it is God's will for us to understand His Word; the Holy Spirit says we are spiritually blinded. He has to remove the veil that blinds you from understanding the truth if you should choose Him. The Holy Bible reveals to us in God's Word, "But their minds were blinded: for until this day remaineth the same veil is done away in Christ" (2 Corinthians 3:14). The Holy Spirit/Spirit of truth is given to the one who believes in Jesus Christ. "Howbeit when he, the Spirit of truth, is come, he will guide you into all truth: for he shall not speak of himself; but whatsoever he shall hear, that shall he speak: and he will shew you things to come" (John 16:13).

> Jesus answered them, I told you, and ye believed not: the works that I do in my Father's name, they bear witness of me. But ye believe not, because ye are not of my sheep, as I said unto you. My sheep hear my voice, and I know them, and they follow me: and I give unto them eternal life, and they shall never perish, neither shall any man pluck them out of my hand. My

Father, which gave them me, is greater than
all; and no man is able to pluck them out of
my Father's hand. I and my Father are one.

John 10:25–30

"Pilate, therefore said unto him, Art thou a king then? Jesus answered, Thou sayest that I am a king. To this end was I born, and for this cause came I into the world, that I should bear witness unto the truth. Every one that is of the truth heareth my voice" (John 18:37). "Jesus answered and said unto him, If a man love me, he will keep my words: and my Father will love him, and we will come unto him, and make our abode with him" (John 14:23). Amen.

If There Is Only One God, Then Why Do We Say Jesus Is God, and Why Do We Say the Holy Ghost/the Holy Spirit Is God Also?

As in the beginning, there was God who lives in heaven, and with Him was the Word, who is Jesus—He is God, and with God was His Holy Spirit/Holy Ghost—He is God, and these three exist as one. The personality of God is three, meaning God the Father, God the Son, and the Holy Spirit of God. The character of God is expressed in three forms: God the Father in heaven, who sits on the throne, God the Son, who was God in the flesh and walked the earth, the Holy Spirit of God/Holy Ghost—God's Spirit. I believe the Holy Spirit of God dwells within the heart of God and contains His love towards us. God's Spirit testifies to the truth, God is a Spirit, and His Spirit dwells in the believers of Jesus Christ. "And without controversy great is the mystery of godliness: God was manifest in the flesh, justified in the Spirit, seen of angels, preached unto the Gentiles, believed on in the world, received up into glory" (1 Timothy 3:16). "What? Know ye not that your body is the temple of the Holy Ghost which is in you, which ye have of God, and ye are not your own" (1 Corinthians 6:19)?

There is no exact example by which one can explain the three manifestations of God, but to come close or even somewhat understand the Three Persons of God, God expresses Himself as three different versions of Himself. God the Father, God the Son, and God the Holy Ghost: these three are one—One God in Three Persons, also known as the Trinity. "And there are differences of administrations, but the same Lord" (1 Corinthians 12:5) "Remember the former things of old: for I am God, and there is none else; I am God, and there is none like Me, Declaring the end from the beginning and from ancient times the things that are not yet done, saying, My counsel shall stand, and I will do all my pleasure" (Isaiah 46:9–10).

For the grace of God that bringeth salvation hath appeared to all men, teaching us that, denying ungodliness and worldly lusts, we should live soberly, righteously, and godly, in this present world; looking for that blessed hope, and the glorious appearing of the great God and our Saviour Jesus Christ; who gave himself for us, that he might redeem us from all iniquity, and purify unto himself a peculiar people, zealous of good works.

Titus 2:11–14

As we see in the scripture above, God has addressed Jesus as "that blessed hope," having something glorious to look forward to, and God has also addressed Jesus as "the Great God and our Savior." So Jesus Christ is God; God said so. Amen.

How Do We Know Jesus Came and Died for Us, and How Can We Be Sure That This Is True?

We know because of the Holy Ghost/Holy Spirit of God. Again, He testifies to the truth, who Jesus is; Jesus said, "I am the way, the truth, and the life." For whosoever has the Holy Spirit of God, this proves that the Scriptures are true, and we, who have the Holy Spirit of God, have received Him/the Holy Spirit of God by the finished work of Jesus on the cross, who died willingly for our sin. God gives to everyone who repents, believes in Jesus/God, and asks the indwelling of the Holy Ghost. "But ye shall receive power, after that, the Holy Ghost is come upon you: and ye shall be witnesses unto me both in Jerusalem, and in all Judaea, and in Samaria, and unto the uttermost part of the earth" (Acts 1:8). "Hereby know we that we dwell in him, and he in us, because he hath given us of his Spirit. And we have seen and do testify that the Father sent the Son to be the Saviour of the world. Whosoever shall confess that Jesus is the Son of God, God dwelleth in him, and he in God" (1 John 4:13–15). "Wherefore I give you to understand, that no man speaking by the Spirit of God calleth Jesus accursed: and that no man can say that Jesus is the Lord, but by the Holy Ghost" (1 Corinthians 12:3). We, therefore, can say what was not understood by Moses and his generation but is now understood to the believers of Jesus Christ because of the indwelling of the Holy Spirit, who is God living in us, amen. In other words, because of Jesus and the finished work on the cross, God is our reality, our truth, and not a mystery.

Father Who Art in Heaven, Why Did It Become Dark at Noon When Our Lord and Savior Was on the Cross?

The Holy Spirit responded, "Daughter, it was then that

Jesus, who is the light of the whole world, took on the many deaths from the sins of the dying world. He cried out to His Father because He felt devastated by the unbearable pain of what it is like to truly be separated from His Father. To die in sin, entering death, separates you from the Father (life), and Jesus did not want to feel separation from His Father because in Him/God is the true pleasures of life. There is no life in death; therefore, Jesus conquered death once and for all to take on the sins of mankind." When we believe in Jesus, we do not have to pay the price of sin; He paid it for us. Amen.

The Holy Spirit also allows us to see in the scriptures, "Now from the sixth hour there was darkness over all the land unto the ninth hour. And about the ninth hour, Jesus cried with a loud voice, saying, Eli, Eli, lama sabachthani? That is to say, My God, my God, why hast thou forsaken me" (Matthew 27:45–46)? As the Holy Spirit continues to give me understanding, Jesus said this because He did not feel His Father's presence in the hours before His death, He felt the excruciating pain from being separated, and He cried out because He did not want to be separated from His Father, but nevertheless, to finish the work on the cross, Jesus became sin for us. He knew no sin and had to enter death to take the keys from death, whereby God has no part in death. God is life, so the presence of God was not there. Jesus shows us in the Scriptures who He is and what He came to do, "Pilate therefore said unto him, Art thou a king then? Jesus answered, Thou sayest that I am a king. To this end was I born, and for this cause came I into the world, that I should bear witness unto the truth. Every one that is of the truth heareth my voice" (John 18:37). "For God so loved the world, that he gave his only begotten Son, that whosoever believeth in him should not perish, but have everlasting life" (John 3:16).

What Are Other Names Used to Refer to the Holy Spirit of God?

The Holy Spirit/Holy Ghost is referred to by more names than these two. The Holy Spirit of God is also called: the Comforter, the Spirit of truth. "But when the Comforter is come, whom I will send unto you from the Father, even the Spirit of truth, which proceedeth from the Father, he shall testify of me" (John 15:26). "Howbeit when he, the Spirit of truth, is come, he will guide you into all truth: for he shall not speak of himself; but whatsoever he shall hear, that shall he speak: and he will shew you things to come. He shall glorify me: for he shall receive of mine, and shall shew it unto you" (John 16:13–14).

The Holy Spirit is also called Another Comforter; Jesus says,

And I will pray the Father, and he shall give you another Comforter, that he may abide with you forever, even the Spirit of truth; whom the world cannot receive, because it seeth him not, neither knoweth him: but ye know him; for He dwelleth with you, and shall be in you. I will not leave you comfortless: I will come to you.

John 14:16–18

What Does Jesus Mean by Another Comforter?

The Holy Spirit says Another Comforter is still the Holy Spirit of God. God the Father has given to us the Holy Spirit of God the right to be with us always and the access through which Jesus can come to us as well. "I am crucified with Christ nevertheless I live; yet not I, but Christ liveth in me: and the life which I now live in the flesh I live by the faith of the Son of God who loved me, and gave himself for me" (Galatians 2:20). The Comforter gives us the right knowledge, and He gives us strength to move forward in all things, including fulfilling the will of God. The Holy Spirit is also referred to as *Paraclete* (Greek) or *Paracletus* (Latin), which means Advocate or Helper. The Holy Spirit is called our Intercessor. "And he that searcheth the hearts knoweth what is the mind of the

Spirit, because he maketh intercession for the saints according to the will of God" (Romans 8:27). "Wherefore he is able also to save them to the uttermost that come unto God by him, seeing he ever liveth to make intercession for them" (Hebrews 7:25).

Although there are many names the Holy Spirit is referred to as; the Holy Spirit instructs me to point out only a few more, which are:

1. *Breath of the All-Mighty*: "The spirit of God hath made me, and the breath of the Almighty hath given me life" (Job 33:4).

2. *Spirit of Counsel*: "And the spirit of the Lord shall rest upon him, the spirit of wisdom and understanding, the spirit of counsel and might, the spirit of knowledge and of the fear of the Lord" (Isaiah 11:2).

3. *Eternal Spirit*: "How much more shall the blood of Christ, who through the eternal Spirit offered himself without spot to God, purge your conscience from dead works to serve the living God" (Hebrews 9:14)?

4. *Power of the Highest*: "And the angel answered and said unto her, The Holy Ghost shall come upon

thee, and the power of the Highest shall overshadow thee: therefore also that holy thing which shall be born of thee shall be called the Son of God" (Luke 1:35).

5. *The Spirit of Adoption*: "For ye have not received the spirit of bondage again to fear; but ye have received the Spirit of adoption, whereby we cry, Abba, Father" (Romans 8:15).

6. *Spirit of Burning*: "When the Lord shall have washed away the filth of the daughters of Zion, and shall have purged the blood of Jerusalem from the midst thereof by the spirit of judgment, and by the spirit of burning" (Isaiah 4:4).

7. *Spirit of Judgment*: "And for a spirit of judgment to him that sitteth in judgment, and for strength to them that turn the battle to the gate" (Isaiah 28:6).

8. *Spirit of Jesus Christ*: "But ye are not in the flesh, but in the Spirit, if so be that the Spirit of God dwell in you. Now if any man have not the Spirit of Christ, he is none of his" (Romans 8:9). "Searching what, or what manner of time the Spirit of Christ which was in them did signify when it testified beforehand the sufferings of Christ, and the glory that

should follow" (1 Peter 1:11).

9. *Spirit of Glory*: "If ye be reproached for the name of Christ, happy are ye; for the spirit of glory and of God resteth upon you: on their part, he is evil spoken of, but on your part, he is glorified" (1 Peter 4:14).

10. *Spirit of Grace*: "And I will pour upon the house of David, and upon the inhabitants of Jerusalem, the spirit of grace and of supplications: and they shall look upon me whom they have pierced, and they shall mourn for him, as one mourneth for his only son, and shall be in bitterness for him, as one that is in bitterness for his firstborn" (Zechariah 12:10).

11. *Spirit of Truth*: "Even the Spirit of truth; whom the world cannot receive, because it seeth him not, neither knoweth him: but ye know him; for he dwelleth with you, and shall be in you" (John 14:17).

12. *Spirit of Life*: "For the law of the Spirit of life in Christ Jesus hath made me free from the law of sin and death" (Romans 8:2).

13. *Spirit of Wisdom*: "That the God of our Lord Jesus Christ, the Father of glory, may give unto you the spirit of wisdom and revelation in the knowledge

of him" (Ephesians 1:17).

14. *Spirit of Knowledge*: "And the spirit of the Lord shall rest upon him, the spirit of wisdom and understanding, the spirit of counsel and might, the spirit of knowledge and of the fear of the Lord" (Isaiah 11:2).

15. *Spirit of the Living God*: "Forasmuch as ye are manifestly declared to be the epistle of Christ ministered by us, written not with ink, but with the Spirit of the living God; not in tables of stone but in fleshly tables of the heart" (2 Corinthians 3:3).

16. *Spirit of Prophecy*: "And I fell at his feet to worship him. And he said unto me, See thou do it not: I am thy fellow servant, and of thy brethren that have the testimony of Jesus: worship God: for the testimony of Jesus is the spirit of prophecy" (Revelation 19:10).

17. *Spirit of the Son*: "And because ye are sons, God hath sent forth the Spirit of his Son into your hearts, crying, Abba, Father" (Galatians 4:6).

Why Did God Point Out the Names by Which His Spirit Is Referred To, and Why Do We Need to Know This?

The Holy Spirit says that because His Spirit is so grand and powerful, it is relevant that we should know by which He is called, that you should have no question of whom dwells in you, to the believer in Christ Jesus first. In knowing all of this about the Holy Spirit of God, we are able to have a better understanding of the heart and mind of God. Here, God illustrates His Word. I believe the Holy Spirit is the very heart of God. To me, the Holy Spirit is God's heart, which is like dynamite (an explosion of love) toward us! Amen.

A dear friend of over thirty years told me that the name Jesus is not the name of God's Son. I decided to look online but first needed to pray to ask the Holy Spirit to direct my path in seeking the appropriate information. I came across a site online called "learnreligion.com." Checking the name of God, to my surprise, but not in this order, I found out that God is Yahweh, which means the Lord is salvation. Yahweh is also Yeshua, which means Savior. So I found out that Yahweh/Yeshua is God's name in Hebrew, but in Greek, God's name is translated from Yeshua to Lesous, and the English name for Lesous is Jesus. The online dictionary says in Latin, the name of Jesus is Iesvs; therefore, the name Jesus is universal. Amen. As the Scriptures have said and are true, there is no other name common to man by which one can be saved.

God's Spirit visited Mary, and He said, "And she shall bring forth a son, and thou shalt call his name Jesus: for he shall save his people from their sins" (Matthew 1:21).

> Wherefore God also hath highly exalted him, and given him a name which is above every name: that at the name of Jesus every knee should bow, of things in heaven, and things in earth, and things under the earth; and that every tongue should confess that Jesus Christ is Lord, to the glory of God the Father.

Philippians 2:9–11

"Neither is there salvation in any other: for there is none other name under heaven given among men, whereby we must be saved" (Acts 4:12). For those who have not the Holy Spirit of God, you still need to know that Jesus is who God says He is.

Was Jesus in the Beginning with God?

And God said, "My people are destroyed for lack of knowledge: because thou hast rejected knowledge, I will also reject thee, that thou shalt be no priest to me: seeing thou hast forgotten the law of thy God, I will also forget thy children" (Hosea 4:6). It is what we do not know that has the ability to do us harm, and the ending thereof will destroy us, having the power to condemn our eternity if we know not and do not keep God's Word. God says, "I have heard the cries of My people, they are in need of Me, I Am that I Am, the God who saves, full of grace and mercy, I will save mankind (My creation)." God said, "I will save My people," meaning that He was our Savior even from the beginning when we prayed to Him, and God sent His Word that He will be with us. I heard the Holy Spirit say, "Remember what was written before: In the beginning was the Word and the Word was with God. The Word was God, and the Word became flesh and dwelt amongst us." God announced this as one word (Emmanuel/God with us), God in the flesh, His name shall be Jesus, and He will save His people. Jesus was the Word with God. Remember when God was creating man, He said, "Let us make man." God was referring to Him and Jesus—man was made after their own image and likeness. Yes, we see that Jesus was in the beginning with God. The scripture says, "In the beginning was the Word, and the Word was with God, and the Word was God" (John 1:1). "And the Word was made flesh, and dwelt among us, (and we beheld his glory, the glory as of the only begotten of the Father,) full of grace and truth" (John 1:14). To me, it's now understood that Jesus is not like man—a creation of God—because He is God who came down from heaven. When God entered the physical world, which He created, He had already placed the laws by which we must abide in order to be legitimate—have occupancy on earth. Those who believe and are called, according to the power that works in them, which is the Holy Spirit from God through Jesus, will know that the Holy Spirit testifies that Jesus is the truth. Jesus points out the origin of the Holy Spirit, "And ye also shall bear witness, because ye have been with me from the beginning" (John 15:27).

Golden Nuggets

- The Holy Spirit of God is always teaching, always testifying to the glory of God in Jesus Christ. The Holy Spirit is moving so fast, in me and through me, sometimes I must be still in order to catch up with Him. Amen.

- "The indwelling Holy Spirit of God continues to perfect our spirit man into the image of Jesus/ God," says the Spirit of truth. Why? Because this is the will of God so that He may be with us and that we might feel His love, which is great towards us, amen. The Holy Spirit, if you did not know, wrote the Holy Bible, and He gives the understanding of the Word of God to those who ask, amen. God says He gives us power, love, and a sound mind, and it is in our best interest to live day by day/one day at a time by His Word, amen. "Give us this day our daily bread" (Matthew 6:11). It is good to ask God daily for our needed portion; whether it be strength, food, or things, we are to seek God every day for it. "But seek ye first the kingdom of God, and his righteousness, and all these things shall be added unto you" (Matthew 6:33). There is no better or greater time than now to seek God/Jesus. I have heard; therefore, I write what the Holy Spirit says:

"A time is coming." We must get prepared! God does not want us to worry because He can help us if we ask Him to. Amen.

Chapter 17

Legitimacy

We (mankind) have the right to exist on the earth; the unseen/spirit realm does not. Three reasons why this is true: 1) God has created mankind from the elements of the seen world (the earth), such as from the dust of the ground, we are authentically from the earth; 2) we are made in God's likeness, in the image of God, and; 3) the breath of God is in us, which gives us life to exist. Our flesh, the breath of God in us, and the Word of God give us authority/legitimacy to be in the earth realm, and anything that is made up of these three consistencies is a gift from God and is a legal resident in the earth realm. Anything that does not have these three consistencies by God is illegitimate or will invade a body to exist in the earth realm. If other beings do not have the legitimacy to be in the earth realm, they do not have God's permission, or His Spirit, His might, or His authority to conquer mankind; therefore, we have hope in the Word of God. Amen.

Why Is This Something of Interest (Legitimacy)?
This is interesting because we must know that we are

invaluable in God's sight and that the attacks on mankind originate from the things that are not seen (from the unseen world, which includes the devil), whereby the devil must possess a body (a person) in order to have the necessary power needed to rule on the earth. His attacks start with influencing the mind (thoughts) and imagination.

The enemy's plan towards God's creation (mankind) always sums up evil. Because the devil is not like us, God's love is not towards him; therefore, he/Satan (the devil) is our worst enemy. God does not lie; He does not break His own will for mankind. So God, because of His faithfulness to His Word and to His creation, entered the earth realm through the womb of a woman, birthed having flesh, became a man, and at the same time, He was God. His plan on the earth was to conquer evil to free the captives (save those who were lost) and reconnect us to Himself. God in heaven (our Father) warns us of the devil's devices that we may know we have a way to escape the enemy, and that way is by the Word (Jesus), who is God,

> And God said, let us make man in our image, after our likeness: and let them have dominion over the fish of the sea, and over the fowl of the air, and over the cattle, and over all the earth, and over every creeping

thing that creepeth upon the earth. So God created man in his own image, in the image of God created he him; male and female created he them. And God blessed them, and God said unto them, Be fruitful, and multiply, and replenish the earth, and subdue it: and have dominion over the fish of the sea, and over the fowl of the air, and over every living thing that moveth upon the earth.

Genesis 1:26–28

"And the Lord God formed man of the dust of the ground, and breathed into his nostrils the breath of life; and man became a living soul" (Genesis 2:7).

When mankind cried out for help to God, God sent an angel with the message to a woman named Mary; she was not clear on the understanding of the message. "And the angel answered and said unto her, The Holy Ghost shall come upon thee, and the power of the Highest shall overshadow thee: therefore, also that holy thing which shall be born of thee shall be called the Son of God" (Luke 1:35). God wants us to know, "Lest Satan should get an advantage of us: for we are not ignorant of his devices" (2 Corinthians 2:11). God also wants us to know, "Now ye are the body of

Christ, and members in particular" (1 Corinthians 12:27). And God is with us, "There hath no temptation taken you but such as is common to man: but God is faithful, who will not suffer you to be tempted above that ye are able; but will with the temptation also make a way to escape, that ye may be able to bear it" (1 Corinthians 10:13). We can escape the devices of Satan/the devil by putting our trust in God, "For with God nothing shall be impossible" (Luke 1:37). Amen.

Golden Nuggets

- Why do we look to another to fulfill all our needs when they cannot? Why do we look for validation in others when we should not? No one can be 100 percent of what we need. We must not look to another to fulfill all our needs; we must look to the Lord, God Almighty.

- I find that life's journey is not simple, it's complex, and therefore, I have carefully considered that my life's journey is so much better with Jesus than without Him.

Amen.

Chapter 18

Jesus (God)

The Holy Spirit of God has said in the beginning, "God said, 'Let us make man in our image after our likeness.'" Going back to Genesis 1:26, the pages beforehand, we said we would point out/speak about who is "us." As we see in John 1:1 and 14, in the beginning, was the Word, and the Word was with God, and the Word was God, and the Word became flesh and walked on the earth. God (Word) and flesh (Emmanuel, meaning God with us); this manifestation of God is from God and by Him. Entering the womb of Mary, He put on flesh, whereby His name is Jesus, who is the Son of God. Therefore "us" is the Word that was with God and is God; yes, the Word became flesh and dwelt among us. As we read previously, His name is Iesvs—meaning, in Latin, Jesus—Yeshua—in Hebrew, referring to Jesus—Lesous—in Greek, meaning Jesus. And all the names above, which refer to Jesus, in English, all are the names which we know to be Jesus/Savior, the manifestation of God, at the same time, being man on earth. "And Pilate wrote a title, and put it on the cross. And the writing was JESUS OF NAZARETH THE KING OF THE JEWS.

This title then read many of the Jews: for the place where Jesus was crucified was nigh to the city: and it was written in Hebrew, and Greek, and Latin" (John 19:19–20).

> And it shall come to pass, that whosoever shall call on the name of the Lord shall be saved. Ye men of Israel, hear these words; Jesus of Nazareth, a man approved of God among you by miracles and wonders and sign, which God did by him in the midst of you, as ye yourselves also know.

Acts 2:21–22

"And it shall come to pass, that whosoever shall call on the name of the Lord shall be delivered: for in mount Zion and in Jerusalem shall be deliverance, as the Lord hath said, and in the remnant whom the Lord shall call" (Joel 2:32).

Jesus is the only Lord of salvation, and He is for us. Remember, we saw in the Bible Jesus was with God as the Word in the beginning. Now you may also know that the Scriptures are true about Jesus (Lord of salvation), who is the Son of God, and God has given all things into His hands, in heaven, on earth, under the earth, and in eternity, amen. In other words, when God was in the flesh and walked with us, some will ask, Why didn't God just call Himself God instead of Jesus, the Son of God? He said "in whom," referring to Jesus, that He is well pleased? "And lo a voice from heaven, saying, This is my beloved Son, in whom I am well pleased" (Matthew 3:17). The Holy Spirit says, "For two reasons." The first example, water is a liquid, but water can also be ice—solid—whereby water's form has changed to meet a particular mandate. Would anyone call ice water when it is solid? Of course not, because that would not be correct; water can also be snow. Can you make a snowman out of water, the liquid? No! Only if the water has changed its form to be snow. So, for example, we can say, "God is water, and He has shown His manifestation"—let's say as ice and as snow. In other words, God being water (our Father in heaven), God being the ice (Jesus), and God being the snow (Holy Spirit). These are some examples that the Holy Spirit has given me. The second reason is that God gave Himself the name that was befitting to the circumstance at hand. Jesus means Savior/Messiah—in Greek, Yeshua—and God said Jesus was His Son because Jesus is from Him; as we see/ understand, the blood of Jesus was the blood of God. We are similar in this aspect concerning the bloodline of the male created by God. For example, the father of the un-born child can always be determined by the blood type of the father. And so, it was correct for God to say Jesus is His Son but fully God and fully man at the same time, on earth. Amen.

Who Is Jesus?

The Holy Spirit of God says Jesus is God in the flesh, who walked on earth as the perfect sacrifice to save mankind and to be the bridge to connect us back to God in heaven. All authority is given to Him, amen. "And all things are of God, who hath reconciled us to himself by Jesus Christ, and hath given to us the ministry of reconciliation; to wit, that God was in Christ, reconciling the world unto himself, not imputing their trespasses unto them; and hath committed unto us the word of reconciliation" (2 Corinthians 5:18–19).

Is Christ the Last Name of Jesus?

Christ is a title and not His last name. It means "Anointed One," as the dictionary reads. God spoke, "I will declare the decree: the Lord hath said unto me, Thou are my Son; this day have I begotten thee" (Psalm 2:7). God is in Jesus; Jesus is God in the flesh. "Looking unto Jesus, the author and finisher of our faith; who for the joy that was set before him endured the cross, despising the shame, and is set down at the right hand of the throne of

God" (Hebrews 12:2).

> In the last day, the great day of the feast,
> Jesus stood and cried, saying, If any man
> thirst, let him come unto me, and drink. He
> that believeth on me, as the scripture hath
> said, out of his belly shall flow rivers of liv-
> ing water. (But this spake he of the Spirit,
> which they that believe on him should re-
> ceive: for the Holy Ghost was not yet given;
> because that Jesus was not yet glorified.)

John 7:37–39

"Nevertheless, I tell you the truth; it is expedient for
you that I go away: for if I go not away, the Comforter
will not come unto you; but if I depart, I will send him
unto you" (John 16:7). "But when the Comforter is come,
whom I will send unto you from the Father, even the Spirit
of truth, which proceedeth from the Father, he shall testify of me" (John 15:26). Jesus says, "And the Holy Spirit,
which is the Comforter, will be able to dwell within you,
and I will be with you." "For he whom God hath sent speaketh the words of God: for God giveth not the Spirit by
measure unto him" (John 3:34). "Seek the Lord and his
strength, seek his face continually" (1 Chronicles 16:11).
God freely gives His Spirit to those who believe and ask;

you can never grow tired of God because the more you seek Him, the more of Him you want.

Why Do We Need the Holy Spirit?

Jesus wants us to know that we need the Holy Spirit to be connected to God, to be in a relationship with Him, that we may know what is true, and to receive the power that sustains us to live on the earth/to do His will. Amen. "But ye shall receive power, after that the Holy Ghost is come upon you: and ye shall be witnesses unto me both in Jerusalem, and in all Judaea, and in Samaria, and unto the uttermost part of the earth" (Acts 1:8). "For as many as are led by the Spirit of God, they are the sons of God" (Romans 8:14). "But if the Spirit of him that raised up Jesus from the dead dwell in you, he that raised up Christ from the dead shall also quicken your mortal bodies by his Spirit that dwelleth in you" (Romans 8:11). "For the Holy Ghost shall teach you in the same hour what ye ought to say" (Luke 12:12).

The Holy Spirit of God/Holy Ghost is given from God. God is the one who anoints the chosen ones and the believers to do His will with power because of the finished work of Jesus on the cross. "But the anointing which ye have received of him abideth in you, and ye need not that any man teach you: but as the same anointing teacheth you of all

174

things and is truth, and is no lie, and even as it hath taught you, ye shall abide in him" (1 John 2:27). Know this, the devil is deceitful and is the accuser of the brethren/believers who can know or recognize his evil ways, except the Holy Spirit, who speaks to us in truth that we should resist and escape the devil by the Word of God and our belief in Jesus Christ. The accuser (devil) sometimes will bring accusations against you/me, telling us that God does not hear us, and the devil reminds us also of our past sins in order to attack our faith because he knows that without faith in God, we can do nothing. Also know, the devil always says the opposite of what you are/who you are because he lies. We need the Holy Spirit of God to overcome the tactics of the devil, for, without the Holy Spirit of God, we cannot even fulfill the will of God and do of His good pleasure. Jesus says, "Verily, verily, I say unto you, He that believeth on me, the works that I do shall he do also; and greater works than these shall he do; because I go unto my Father" (John 14:12). As we know, because Jesus went to God the Father, that He may send the Holy Spirit back to us, that He might help us do great things for the kingdom of God, and that we may know the glorious and deep things of the heart and mind of God, without the Holy Spirit, we are vulnerable, and we are limited in being able to do great things for God. Also, we cannot know or receive or even enter the things that pertain to the kingdom of God.

But How Can We Do Greater Things than Jesus?

> The Revelation of Jesus Christ, which God gave unto him, to shew unto his servant's things which must shortly come to pass; and he sent and signified it by his angel unto his servant John: who bare record of the word of God, and of the testimony of Jesus Christ, and of all things that he saw. Blessed is he that readeth, and they that hear the words of this prophecy, and keep those things which are written therein: for the time is at hand.

Revelation 1:1–3

He wants us to know how much we matter in the kingdom of God; He has delegated power and authority to us to have dominion over. "And the kingdom and dominion, and the greatness of the kingdom under the whole heaven shall be given to the people of the saints of the Most High, whose kingdom is an everlasting kingdom, and all dominions shall serve and obey him" (Daniel 7:27). With the Holy Spirit, Jesus said, "Greater works will we do because I will go to the Father and ask Him to send you the Holy

Spirit/the Comforter, who will live in the believer of Jesus Christ, who is greater than the enemy in the world." Every Holy-Ghost-filled believer, along with Jesus in heaven, will do great things because Jesus said He would pray to the Father on our behalf—be our advocate in heaven. "Greater works shall you do because the Holy Spirit and Jesus are with you," this declares what Jesus says is true.

When Jesus walked the earth, He was able to reach many people for the glory of God, but now because of the Holy-Ghost-filled believers who are positioned in every part of the world, we who are in Christ Jesus and filled with the Holy Spirit are able to reach the *whole world* to preach the gospel of Jesus Christ, God, being everywhere at the same time, and see the manifestation of God on the earth, through His power, experiencing miracles and blessings because of His grace, through the believers of Jesus Christ. Amen.

> But God hath revealed them unto us by his Spirit: for the Spirit searcheth all things, yea, the deep things of God. For what man knoweth the things of a man, save the spirit of man which is in him? even so the things of God knoweth no man, but the Spirit of God.

Now we have received, not the spirit of the world, but the spirit which is of God; that we might know the things that are freely given to us of God. Which things also we speak, not in the words which man's wisdom teacheth, but which the Holy Ghost teacheth; comparing spiritual things with spiritual. But the natural man received not the things of the Spirit of God: for they are foolishness unto him: neither can he know them, because they are spiritually discerned. But he that is spiritual judgeth all things, yet he himself is judged of no man. For who hath known the mind of the Lord, that he may instruct him? But we have the mind of Christ.

1 Corinthians 2:10–16

Also, through God's Spirit, "Who hath delivered us from the power of darkness, and hath translated us into the kingdom of his dear Son" (Colossians 1:13).

The Holy Spirit leads us out of the darkness/evil in this world. We need the Holy Spirit to overcome evil, to truly know God, and to live the abundant life Jesus came to give. Amen. God has prepared our bodies to receive Him already, "In whom ye also are builded together for an habitation of God through the Spirit" (Ephesians 2:22).

Therefore my heart is glad, and my glory rejoiceth: my flesh also shall rest in hope. For thou wilt not leave my soul in hell; neither wilt thou suffer thine Holy One to see corruption. Thou wilt shew me the path of life: in thy presence is fulness of joy; at thy right hand there are pleasures for evermore.

Psalm 16:9–11

Looking for the blessed hope and the glorious appearing of the great God and our Saviour Jesus Christ; who gave himself for us, that he might redeem us from all iniquity and purify unto himself a peculiar people, zealous of good works. These things speak and exhort and rebuke with all authority. Let no man despise thee.

Titus 2:13–15

"Having therefore these promises, dearly beloved, let us cleanse ourselves from all filthiness of the flesh and spirit, perfecting holiness in the fear of God" (2 Corinthians 7:1).

We are born into sin, not because we have ever sinned before but because the world is in sin; therefore, we are in sin when we are born because we have not chosen to be righteous or unrighteous yet. If any has not chosen, they are in sin already, which started from the fall of Adam and Eve. There are two masters: 1) God All Mighty—the one who is good/full of grace and mercy; 2) the other—the devil, who is evil/sinful. "And if it seems evil unto you to serve the Lord, choose you this day whom ye will serve; whether the gods which your fathers served that were on the other side of the flood or the gods of the Amorites, in whose land ye dwell: but as for me and my house, we will serve the Lord" (Joshua 24:15). "No man can serve two masters: for either he will hate the one and love the other; or else he will hold to the one, and despise the other. Ye cannot serve God and mammon" (Matthew 6:24). "Behold, I was shapen in iniquity and in sin did my mother conceive me" (Psalm 51:5).

> Nevertheless the foundation of God standeth sure, having this seal, The Lord knoweth them that are his. And, let every one that nameth the name of Christ depart from iniquity. If a man therefore purge himself from these, he shall be a vessel unto honour, sanctified, and meet for the mas-

ter's use, and prepared unto every good
work.

2 Timothy 2:19, 21

"But your iniquities have separated between you and
your God and your sins have hid his face from you, that
he will not hear" (Isaiah 59:2). "He that covereth his sins
shall not prosper: but whoso confesseth and forsaketh them
shall have mercy" (Proverbs 28:13). "But if ye will not do
so, behold, ye have sinned against the Lord: and be sure
your sin will find you out" (Numbers 32:23). "My little
children, these things write I unto you, that ye sin not. And
if any man sin, we have an advocate with the Father, Jesus
Christ the righteous" (1 John 2:1).

We must choose who we will serve. Know that no one
will be able to alter your choice without your consent, for
our Lord has given us this right. "Brethren, I speak after
the manner of men; Though it be but a man's covenant, yet
if it be confirmed, no man disannulleth, or addeth thereto"
(Galatians 3:15). "Stand fast therefore in the liberty where-
with Christ hath made us free, and be not entangled again
with the yoke of bondage" (Galatians 5:1).

Who Does God Say We Are?
"For we are his workmanship, created in Christ Jesus

unto good works, which God hath before ordained that we should walk in them" (Ephesians 2:10). "Now the God of hope fill you with all joy and peace in believing, that ye may abound in hope, through the power of the Holy Ghost" (Romans 15:13). "And hope maketh not ashamed; because the love of God is shed abroad in our hearts by the Holy Ghost which is given unto us" (Romans 5:5). "What? know ye not that your body is the temple of the Holy Ghost which is in you, which ye have of God, and ye are not your own" (1 Corinthians 6:19)?

How Do We Do the Will of God According to His Plan for Us?

"But the Comforter, which is the Holy Ghost, whom the Father will send in my name, he shall teach you all things, and bring all things to your remembrance, whatsoever I have said unto you" (John 14:26). How does God bring all things to remembrance? We must renew our minds. "And be not conformed to this world: but be ye transformed by the renewing of your mind, that ye may prove what is that good, and acceptable, and perfect, will of God" (Romans 12:2). According to the Holy Spirit, what does renew mean? Renew is to replenish/refresh our minds. "Study to shew thyself approved unto God, a workman that needeth not to be ashamed, rightly dividing the word of truth"

(2 Timothy 2:15). "Beloved, if our heart condemn us not, then have we confidence toward God. And whatsoever we ask, we receive of him, because we keep his commandments, and do those things that are pleasing in his sight" (1 John 3:21–22). "Likewise, the Spirit also helpeth our infirmities: for we know not what we should pray for as we ought: but the Spirit itself maketh intercession for us with groanings which cannot be uttered" (Romans 8:26). "And the spirit of the Lord shall rest upon him, the spirit of wisdom and understanding, the spirit of counsel and might, the spirit of knowledge and of the fear of the Lord" (Isaiah 11:2).

What Is the Fear of the Lord? Why Should We Fear God?

"The fear of the Lord is the beginning of wisdom: and the knowledge of the holy is understanding" (Proverbs 9:10). "The fear of the Lord is the beginning of knowledge: but fools despise wisdom and instruction" (Proverbs 1:7). "The fear of the Lord is to hate evil: pride, and arrogance, and the evil way, and the froward mouth, do I hate" (Proverbs 8:13).

> And the Lord spake unto Moses, saying,
> Speak unto the children of Israel, and say
> unto them, I am the Lord your God. After

the doings of the land of Egypt, wherein ye dwelt, shall ye not do: and after the doings of the land of Canaan, whither I bring you, shall ye not do: neither shall ye walk in their ordinances. Ye shall do my judgments, and keep mine ordinances, to walk therein: I am the Lord your God. Ye shall therefore keep my statutes, and my judgments: which if a man do, he shall live in them: I am the Lord. None of you shall approach to any that is near of kin to him, to uncover their nakedness: I am the Lord. The nakedness of thy father, or the nakedness of thy mother, shalt not uncover: she is thy mother; thou shalt not uncover her nakedness. The nakedness of thy father's wife shalt thou not uncover: it is thy father's nakedness. The nakedness of thy sister, the daughter of thy father, or daughter of thy mother, whether she be born at home, or born abroad, even their nakedness thou shalt not uncover. The nakedness of thy son's daughter, or of thy daughter's daughter, even their nakedness thou shalt not uncover: for theirs is thine own nakedness. The nakedness of thy father's wife's daughter, begotten of the father, she is thy sister, thou shalt not uncover

184

her nakedness. Thou shalt not uncover the nakedness of thy father's sister: she is thy father's near kinswoman. Thou shalt not uncover the nakedness of thy mother's sister: for she is thy mother's near kinswoman. Thou shalt not uncover the nakedness of thy father's brother, thou shalt not approach to his wife: she is thine aunt. Thou shalt not uncover the nakedness of thy daughter in law: she is thy son's wife; thou shalt not uncover her nakedness. Thou shalt not uncover the nakedness of thy brother's wife: it is thy brother's nakedness. Thou shalt not uncover the nakedness of a woman and her daughter, neither shalt thou take her son's daughter, or her daughter's daughter, to uncover her nakedness; for they are her near kinswomen: it is wickedness. Neither shalt thou take a wife to her sister, to vex her, to uncover her nakedness, beside the other in her lifetime. Also thou shalt not approach unto a woman to uncover her nakedness, as long as she is put apart for her uncleanness. Moreover, thou shalt not lie carnally with thy neighbour's wife, to defile thyself with her. And thou shalt not let any of thy seed pass through the fire to Molech, neither shalt thou profane the name of thy God: I am the Lord. Thou shalt not lie with mankind, as with womankind: it is abomination. Neither shalt thou lie with any beast to defile thyself therewith: neither shall any woman stand before a beast to lie down thereto: it is confusion. Defile not ye yourselves in any of these things: for in all these the nations are defiled which I cast out before you: and the land is defiled: therefore, I do visit the iniquity thereof upon it, and the land itself vomiteth out her inhabitants. Ye shall therefore keep my statutes and my judgments, and shall not commit any of these abominations; neither any of your own nation, nor any stranger that sojourneth among you: (for all these abominations have the men of the land done, which were before you, and the land is defiled;) that the land spue not you out also, when ye defile it, as it spued out the nations that were before you. For whosoever shall commit any of these abominations, even the souls that commit them shall be cut off from among their people. Therefore shall ye keep mine ordinance, that ye commit not any one of these abominable customs, which were commit-

ted before you, and that ye defile not yourselves therein: I am the Lord your God.

Leviticus 18:1–30

The Holy Spirit says that because of those who have
already done what is against the will of God, they have
caused the land to spew them out/to reject them. God says,
"In the fear of the Lord is strong confidence: and his children shall have a place of refuge" (Proverbs 14:26). "By
humility and the fear of the Lord are riches, and honour,
and life" (Proverbs 22:4). "Let all the earth fear the Lord:
let all the inhabitants of the world stand in awe of him"
(Psalm 33:8). "The secret of the Lord is with them that
fear him; and he will shew them his covenant" (Psalm
25:14). "The fear of the Lord tendeth to life: and he that
hath it shall abide satisfied; he shall not be visited with
evil" (Proverbs 19:23). We should fear God because, "Let
us hear the conclusion of the whole matter: Fear God, and
keep his commandments: for this is the whole duty of
man" (Ecclesiastes 12:13). As we see, the fear of the Lord
is good, and a good fear is called righteous fear, but there
is also a fear that is not good; it is of evil, and this fear is
called the unrighteous fear.

Righteous Fear versus Unrighteous Fear
There is a healthy/righteous fear, which is good, and

there is an unhealthy/unrighteous fear, which is bad. Righteous fear helps you to understand and moves you toward better—it helps you to progress. Unrighteous fear makes you disabled, keeping you ignorant of the truth. It stops you from progressing. For example, the difference in healthy fear commands you to be respectful, to act, or go forth with enthusiasm; for instance, as we quoted before, the fear of the Lord is the beginning of wisdom, etc. Healthy fear gives you strength to do what you wouldn't do ordinarily, whereby unhealthy fear makes you afraid because it torments and eventually destroys you. We must now decide because, ultimately, we are the master of what we choose; we must choose between which fear we will let rule over us, righteous versus unrighteous fear. I choose righteous fear because it is God's will.

What about Fear?

Let's take a look at unrighteous fear. Why does God say over and over again, "Do not be afraid"? God says in the Holy Bible three hundred and sixty-five (365) times and more, "Do not fear." Fear is a thief; fear is a tormenting thief; fear comes to stop you from your purpose; fear paralyzes you from moving towards your calling; fear is a deceiver—it makes you believe that the truth is a lie; fear inhibits the truth; fear does not want you to move forward;

fear deteriorates your character; fear destroys you from the inside out. Fear is most powerful when we focus/think on it constantly because it can take over our imagination, creating intrusive thoughts and causing instability/doubt.

Who Is Fear?

Fear is the enemy of the righteousness in Christ Jesus. Fear opens the door to all kinds of evil spirits. Fear is destruction, a destroyer of what is true. As it was stated above, righteous fear versus unrighteous fear—this, you must know—but there is a righteous fear, which you must have in order to fully serve God. Amen. "The fear of the Lord is a fountain to life, to depart from the snares of death" (Proverbs 14:27). Some preachers/people have said, "If you are afraid to do something, do it anyway—do it afraid." The Holy Spirit says, "Be not be deceived; God is not mocked: for whatsoever a man soweth, that shall he also reap" (Galatians 6:7). Therefore, I say, Do not be afraid, do not fear, because being afraid opens the door to another spirit, and if you are doing anything afraid, you are doing things in your own strength by another spirit and driven not by the Spirit of truth (who is God).

God knows that sometimes we are afraid. He also wants us to know we do not have to be because we can trust in Him. "He will keep the feet of his saints, and the wicked shall be silent in darkness; for by strength shall no man prevail" (1 Samuel 2:9). "Then he answered and spake unto me, saying, This is the word of the Lord unto Zerubbabel, saying, Not by might, nor by power, but by my spirit, saith the Lord of hosts" (Zechariah 4:6). When we trust in God's might, we lean not on our own under-standing. But God directs our paths; wherever we may go, we should know that He is with us, God's power can go ev-erywhere, and He said He would never forsake us. You are not alone, and "The Lord shall fight for you, and ye shall hold your peace" (Exodus 14:14). We can always count on God if we put our complete trust in Him. Amen. "Trust in the Lord with all thine heart; and lean not unto thine own understanding. In all thy ways acknowledge him, and he shall direct thy paths" (Proverbs 3:5–6).

What Is Perfect Love, and Why Do We Need It?

The Holy Spirit says perfect love is the agape love which is the highest form of love towards mankind from God. Everything about this kind of love is perfect, pure, un-conditional, holy, unique, powerful, and so much more. We need this type of love because it is sufficient in all things.

What Then Can Take Away All Fear?

"There is no fear in love; but perfect love casteth out

fear: because fear hath torment. He that feareth is not made perfect in love" (1 John 4:18). "Finally, my brethren, be strong in the Lord, and in the power of his might" (Ephesians 6:10). "I sought the Lord, and he heard me, and delivered me from all my fears" (Psalm 34:4). Because I love God and trust in Him. God said, "Have not I commanded thee? Be strong and of a good courage; be not afraid, neither be thou dismayed: for the Lord thy God is with thee whithersoever thou goest" (Joshua 1:9). Did you not know that being afraid opens up doors to all kinds of evil spirits that are not of Him, such as anxiety, depression, immobility, panic disorders, and many more kinds of spirits that are against the will of God for our life? "Take heed, those who are against My Word are of iniquity, which is against Me (the Lord God Almighty)," "And then will I profess unto them, I never knew you: depart from me, ye that work iniquity" (Matthew 7:23). "The house of the wicked shall be overthrown: but the tabernacle of the upright shall flourish. There is a way which seemeth right unto a man, but the end thereof are the ways of death" (Proverbs 14:11–12).

> Bless the Lord, O my soul, and forget not all His benefits: Who forgiveth all thine iniquities; who healeth all thy diseases; Who redeemeth thy life from destruction; who

crowneth thee with lovingkindness and tender mercies; who satisfieth thy mouth with
good things; so that thy youth is renewed
like the eagle's.

Psalm 103:2–5

"For whom the Lord loveth he correcteth; even as a father the son in whom he delighteth" (Proverbs 3:12). "For
whom the Lord loveth he chasteneth, and scourgeth every son whom he receiveth. If ye endure chastening, God
dealeth with you as with sons; for what son is he whom the
father chasteneth not" (Hebrews 12:6–7)?

Who Then Will You Listen To, Man or God?

"That your faith should not stand in the wisdom of men,
but in the power of God" (1 Corinthians 2:5). "Be not deceived; God is not mocked: for whatsoever a man soweth,
that shall he also reap. For he that soweth to his flesh shall
of the flesh reap corruption; but he that soweth to the Spirit
shall of the Spirit reap life everlasting" (Galatians 6:7–8).

We must take heed and be careful to do what the Word
of God says. "For God hath not given us the spirit of fear,
but of power, and of love, and of a sound mind" (2 Timothy
1:7). Now, we know we cannot operate in fear unless it
is the fear of God, which, then, we are giving honor and

glory to God. Amen. The Holy Spirit says, "Fear thou not; for I am with thee: be not dismayed; for I am thy God: I will strengthen thee; yea, I will help thee; yea, I will uphold thee with the right hand of my righteousness" (Isaiah 41:10). "Thou wilt keep him in perfect peace, whose mind is stayed on thee: because he trusteth in thee" (Isaiah 26:3). "Peace I leave with you, my peace I give unto you: not as the world giveth, give I unto you. Let not your heart be troubled, neither let it be afraid" (John 14:27). "Be careful for nothing; but in everything by prayer and supplication with thanksgiving let your request be made known unto God. And the peace of God, which passeth all understanding, shall keep your hearts and minds through Christ Jesus" (Philippians 4:6–7).

> But now thus saith the Lord that created thee, O Jacob, and he that formed thee, O Israel, Fear not: for I have redeemed thee, I have called thee by thy name; thou art mine. When thou passest through the waters, I will be with thee; and through the rivers, they shall not overflow thee: when thou walkest through the fire, thou shalt not be burned; neither shall the flame kindle upon thee. For I am the Lord thy God, the Holy One of Israel, thy Saviour: I gave Egypt for

thy ransom, Ethiopia and Seba for thee.

Isaiah 43:1–3

"The Lord thy God in the midst of thee is mighty; he will save, he will rejoice over thee with joy; he will rest in his love, he will joy over thee with singing" (Zephaniah 3:17). "Be not afraid of sudden fear, neither of the desolation of the wicked, when it cometh. For the Lord shall be thy confidence, and shall keep thy foot from being taken" (Proverbs 3:25–26). "I sought the Lord, and he heard me, and delivered me from all my fears" (Psalm 34:4). We see that "The fear of the Lord is clean, enduring forever: the judgments of the Lord are true and righteous altogether" (Psalm 19:9). "Nay, in all these things we are more than conquerors through him that loved us" (Romans 8:37).

We understand that God gives us what we ask, according to His will, through the power of the Holy Spirit, who is in us, and according to our faith in His Word. "Now unto Him that is able to do exceeding abundantly above all that we ask or think, according to the power that worketh in us" (Ephesians 3:20). "And he said unto them, Unto you it is given to know the mystery of the kingdom of God: but unto them that are without, all these things are done in parables" (Mark 4:11).

Jesus Spoke in Parables; What Are Parables?

The Holy Spirit says parables are stories that explain what Jesus is speaking about, and the understanding of the story is given to the true believers of Christ who have the Holy Spirit of God living on the inside.

Who Is the Holy Spirit?

On the cross, Jesus gave the Ghost/Holy Spirit of God up to God the Father in heaven for us, the believers. Then God sent the Holy Spirit to all the believers of Jesus, that we may be in Him and He in us. The Holy Spirit is the One who gives the believers direct access to God the Father and Jesus the Christ and vice versa, so that the believers may be with God and Jesus, so that God and Jesus may be with the believers. As the Holy Spirit teaches me, He is the seal from God and the gate by which one can enter heaven, all because of Jesus, amen.

How Do We Receive the Holy Spirit of God?

We must turn from our ways (repent), receive Jesus as our Lord and Savior, then ask God the Father for forgiveness so that we may receive the Holy Spirit in Jesus' name. Amen. "Then Peter said unto them, Repent, and be baptized every one of you in the name of Jesus Christ for the remission of sins, and ye shall receive the gift of the

Holy Ghost" (Acts 2:38).

Where Did the Holy Ghost Come From? What Was the Original Purpose of the Holy Spirit in the Earth Realm?

The Holy Ghost came from God in heaven, who sits on the throne. Again, He is God's Spirit. The Spirit of God was given to Jesus of Nazareth while on earth so that He would have legal power while in the flesh to do the will of God, which is to do good, carrying out His ministry, returning us back to God, healing the sick, and setting the captives free from the devil—our enemy. "How God anointed Jesus of Nazareth with the Holy Ghost and with power: who went about doing good and healing all that were oppressed of the devil; for God was with him" (Acts 10:38). We, therefore, see that the Holy Bible is the truth and the Word of God; we could believe it. Amen. "But we have this treasure in earthen vessels, that the excellency of the power may be of God, and not of us" (2 Corinthians 4:7). "For our gospel came not unto you in word only, but also in power, and in the Holy Ghost, and in much assurance; as we know what manner of men we were among you for your sake" (1 Thessalonians 1:5).

The Holy Ghost says, If you want to see the kingdom of God, if you want to enter the kingdom of God, you must be born again. To be born again, you must be baptized of

196

the Father, of the Son, and of the Holy Spirit of God, and with water, in the Name of Jesus. Amen. "Jesus answered, Verily, verily, I say unto thee, Except a man be born of water and of the Spirit, he cannot enter into the kingdom of God" (John 3:5). The baptism is symbolic of the death of Jesus; the coming up out of the water symbolizes the resurrection of Jesus. The water is symbolic of setting yourself apart from the world, to being holy for God, and it is also accepting the Spirit of God through Jesus Christ and wholeheartedly confessing that Jesus is Lord. Amen. "Because it is written, Be ye holy; for I am holy" (1 Peter 1:16).

> Therefore we are buried with him by baptism into death: that like as Christ was raised up from the dead by the glory of the Father, even so, we also should walk in newness of life. For if we have been planted together in the likeness of his death, we shall be also in the likeness of his resurrection: knowing this, that our old man is crucified with him, that the body of sin might be destroyed, that henceforth we should not serve sin.

Romans 6:4–6

In other words, Jesus' death represents so much.

When we accept Jesus as our Savior by faith, His death buried our sin/destroyed it, and His resurrection represents our new man/body, which is no longer under the law of sin; our new life is in Christ. To me, to be born again is to have a new life in Christ. "If ye were of the world, the world would love his own: but because ye are not of the world, but I have chosen you out of the world, therefore the world hateth you" (John 15:19). Jesus wants us to know not to be worried because we don't fit in; He has chosen us to stand out for the glory of God in Him; we are not of the world as He is not either. Amen.

Why Does the Bible Say "Though We Live in the World, We Are Not of the World"?

Jesus explains to the believers, "They are not of the world, even as I am not of the world" (John 17:16). "And have no fellowship with the unfruitful works of darkness, but rather reprove them" (Ephesians 5:11).

"For our conversation is in heaven; from whence also we look for the Saviour, the Lord Jesus Christ" (Philippians 3:20). Amen.

Golden Nugget

- God says heaven is before us. Heaven awaits us; the doors of heaven are open and are waiting to receive all those who believe in the Son of God. We cannot stay focused on the things of this world because it is passing away, and it is not perfect; if it were, it would be heaven. Set your mind on the things above. "Set your affection on things above, not on things on the earth" (Colossians 3:2). We must all come into repentance. Amen.

Chapter 19

The Importance of Jesus' Death

Why Did Jesus Die for Us?

The Holy Spirit teaches me that the death of Jesus was to set the captives free, those who are under the law/fallen away/fell short of the glory of God. Jesus, therefore, had to pay the price so that we would not pay in order to reclaim the lost souls, meaning because of sin in the world, many walk in darkness and are lost (dead) in Jesus Christ. Because of what Adam and Eve did, this world is not our home; it is not perfect. God, "Who hath delivered us from the power of darkness, and hath translated us into the kingdom of his dear Son" (Colossians 1:13). "Then spake Jesus again unto them saying, I am the light of the world: he that followeth me shall not walk in darkness, but shall have the light of life" (John 8:12). There is but One who has all power and authority to save the lost; He is Jesus Christ our Lord. God, who has commanded His love towards us, did not fail to leave us hopeless.

In God's compassion towards us, He became the perfect gift to the world to reconcile us back to Himself, where we belong. Thus far, the Scriptures say that God's Spirit entered the womb of the woman named Mary, and she birthed Emmanuel, meaning God is with us, and His name would be Jesus—Wonderful Savior. He would save His people, the ones who believe in Him. The beauty in the death of Jesus was that God in heaven, our Father, has compassion for His creation because He cares much and commanded His unconditional love towards us through His beloved Son. We mean everything to God; He gave up His life so that we may live. The importance of Jesus' death, as God shows us, is that it lets us take a look into the mind of God, seeing how much He loves mankind. Through the death of Jesus on the cross, God declared that His Son is given all power and authority in heaven, on earth, under the earth, and in eternity. At His Name, every knee shall bow. Death/sin/the law are all under the feet of Jesus Christ, meaning under His power.

In order for the work of Jesus to be complete, Jesus died for us so that He may do away with the law, also re-move/take the keys of death, rendering death powerless, and bringing everything under the authority of Jesus Christ the Lord. Therefore, to the believers in Christ, to the ones who are called and love God, the Holy Spirit says we shall not fear death, Jesus has overcome death, and He holds the keys. Know that our lives are in His hands; death cannot claim us unless we willingly give in. Jesus/God determines our future when we choose to obey Him; He promises us life and to have it more abundantly. We must not give in to death or give up on life. Believe the Word of God, that by His stripes, we were already healed from all things, including sin. All things that are against God's will for us are sickness/disease; that is why He tells us we can be healed/saved from all things; His dying on the cross was the price that He was willing to pay for us so that we would not have to pay for our own sin if we truly obey God's will. God's intentions towards us are always for our good. God wants us to know not to fear the evils of this world but put all our trust in Him—the God of Abraham, Isaac, and Jacob. God speaks, "I Am Alpha & Omega—the Almighty God who sits on the throne, Good/Holy." "And Jesus came and spake unto them, saying, All power is given unto me in heaven and in earth" (Matthew 28:18). "That at the name of Jesus every knee should bow, of things in heaven, and things in earth, and things under the earth and that every tongue should confess that Jesus Christ is Lord, to the glory of God the Father" (Philippians 2:10–11).

No matter what it looks like or may appear to be like or what life brings, there is nothing/no one more powerful or greater than God/Jesus. Always believe that by His stripes, His shed blood, and in His Name, having faith, that all things are possible. "But that no man is justified by the law in the sight of God, it is evident: for, The just shall live by faith. And the law is not of faith: but, The man that doeth them shall live in them" (Galatians 3:11–12). "Verily I say unto thee, Thou shalt by no means come out thence, till thou hast paid the uttermost farthing" (Matthew 5:26). "For ye are bought with a price: therefore glorify God in your body, and in your spirit, which are God's" (1 Corinthians 6:20). "Look unto Jesus the author and finisher of our faith; who for the joy that was set before him endured the cross, despising the shame, and is set down at the right hand of the throne of God" (Hebrews 12:2). God speaks, saying, "I am the God of Abraham, and the God of Isaac, and the God of Jacob? God is not the God of the dead, but of the living" (Matthew 22:32). "I am Alpha and Omega, the beginning and the ending, saith the Lord, which is, and which was, and which is to come, the Almighty" (Revelation 1:8). Jesus speaks, "And he said unto him, Why callest thou me good? There is none good but one, that is, God: but if thou wilt enter into life, keep the commandments" (Matthew 19:17). "There is none holy as the Lord: for there is none beside thee: neither is there any rock like our God" (1 Samuel 2:2). "Because it is written, Be ye holy; for I am holy (1 Peter 1:16). "Jesus knowing that the Father had given all things into his hands and that he was come from God, and went to God" (John 13:3).

The importance of Jesus' death, as He explains, "Jesus said unto her, I am the resurrection, and the life: he that believeth in me, though he were dead, yet shall he live and whosoever liveth and believeth in me shall never die. Believest thou this" (John 11:25–26)? "My kingdom is not of this world," as Jesus said. The Holy Spirit says that in order to have the life God intended for mankind, we must repent—turn from our ways, believe in the Son of God, and we must be born again. This means that you must be baptized with water and of the Spirit of God in order to enter into the kingdom of God (having all that God has promised through Jesus).

God says (that Jesus), "But he was wounded for our transgressions, he was bruised for our iniquities: the chastisement of our peace was upon him; and with his stripes we are healed" (Isaiah 53:5). "Verily, verily, I say unto you, Except a corn of wheat fall into the ground and die, it abideth alone: but if it die, it bringeth forth much fruit" (John 12:24). "But if we walk in the light, as he is in the light, we have fellowship one with another, and the blood of Jesus Christ his Son cleanseth us from all sin" (1 John 1:7). "For with God nothing shall be impossible" (Luke 1:37). "For whatsoever is born of God overcometh the world: and this is the victory that overcometh the world, even our faith" (1 John 5:4). Amen.

Why Is the Blood of Jesus So Relevant?

The blood of Jesus is so relevant because it finalizes an agreement concerning the price needed to be paid that speaks and bears witness to the power of Jesus to cleanse us from sin, saving us from the wrath of God, and giving the believer the abundance of life. His blood is multipurpose—sacred (uniquely holy), sacrificial, and so much more, "For the life of the flesh is in the blood: and I have given it to you upon the altar to make an atonement for your souls: for it is the blood that maketh an atonement for the soul" (Leviticus 17:11). "For this is my blood of the new testament, which is shed for many for the remission of sins" (Matthew 26:28). "But if we walk in the light, as he is in the light, we have fellowship one with another, and the blood of Jesus Christ his Son cleanseth us from all sin" (1 John 1:7). "In whom we have redemption through his blood, the forgiveness of sins, according to the riches of his grace" (Ephesians 1:7). "And from Jesus Christ, who is the faithful witness, and the first begotten of the dead, and the prince of the kings of the earth. Unto him that loved us, and washed us from our sins in his own blood" (Revelation

1:5). "Having therefore, brethren, boldness to enter into the holiest by the blood of Jesus" (Hebrews 10:19). "Much more then, being now justified by his blood, we shall be saved from wrath through him" (Romans 5:9). "How much more shall the blood of Christ, who through the eternal Spirit offered himself without spot to God, purge your conscience from dead works to serve the living God" (Hebrews 9:14)?

God wants us to know that the Blood speaks. God shows us in the scriptures, "And Cain talked with Abel his brother: and it came to pass, when they were in the field, that Cain rose up against Abel his brother, and slew him. And the Lord said unto Cain, Where is Abel thy brother" (Genesis 4:8–9)? "And he said, 'What hast thou done?' The voice of thy brother's blood crieth unto me from the ground" (Genesis 4:10). "And to Jesus the mediator of the new covenant, and to the blood of sprinkling, that speaketh better things than that of Abel" (Hebrews 12:24). "And almost all things are by the law purged with blood: and without shedding of blood is no remission" (Hebrews 9:22). "For Christ is not entered into the holy places made with hands, which are the figures of the true; but into heaven itself, now to appear in the presence of God for us" (Hebrews 9:24). "Herein is love, not that we loved God, but that he loved us, and sent his Son to be the propitiation for our sins" (1 John 4:10). "But now being made free from sin, and become servants to God, ye have your fruit unto holiness, and the end everlasting life. For the wages of sin is death; but the gift of God is eternal life through Jesus Christ our Lord" (Romans 6:22–23). "If any man see his brother sin a sin which is not unto death, he shall ask, and he shall give him life for them that sin not unto death. There is a sin unto death: I do not say that he shall pray for it. All unrighteousness is sin: and there is a sin not unto death" (1 John 5:16–17).

The Holy Spirit instructs me that all sin is unrighteous/ ungodly, and the sin that is not unto death is when you repent of sin, but the sin that is unto death is when you do not repent, unrepented sin is unto death. "I tell you, Nay: but, except ye repent, ye shall all likewise perish" (Luke 13:3). God wants us to repent, "For the wrath of God is revealed from heaven against all ungodliness and unrighteousness of men, who hold the truth in unrighteousness" (Romans 1:18).

> But unto them that are contentious, and do not obey the truth, but obey unrighteousness, indignation, and wrath, tribulation and anguish, upon every soul of man that doeth evil, of the Jew first, and also of the

Gentile; but glory, honour, and peace, to every man that worketh good, to the Jew first, and also to the Gentile: for there is no respect of persons with God.

Romans 2:8–11

How Do We Overcome the Devil?

And I heard a loud voice saying in heaven, Now is come salvation, and strength, and the kingdom of our God, and the power of his Christ: for the accuser of our brethren is cast down, which accused them before our God day and night. And they overcome him by the blood of the Lamb, and by the word of their testimony; and they loved not their lives unto the death.

Revelation 12:10–11

Jesus prayed for us, "Then said Jesus, Father, forgive them; for they know not what they do. And they parted his raiment, and cast lots" (Luke 23:34). "Jesus answered and said unto them, Destroy this temple, and in three days I will raise it up" (John 2:19).

What Does This Scripture Mean?

The Holy Spirit teaches me that Jesus was telling those around Him about the future, which involved Himself. The temple, which was God in the flesh (Jesus), "Saying, The Son of man must be delivered into the hands of sinful men, and be crucified, and the third day rise again" (Luke 24:7). "And said unto them, Thus it is written, and thus it beloved Christ to suffer, and to rise from the dead the third day" (Luke 24:46). Jesus was not speaking about a building when He said temple, but He was speaking about His body.

The point of mentioning this scripture is that, like before, in the days that Jesus spoke, He told us of what was to come so that we would be prepared/believe and not be in shock or ignorant in what's to come. We are being told even now, by the same God who spoke back then, to be prepared for a time that is coming that will be unbearable. God says, "Seek Me and live," reminding us that for those who truly love God, He dwells in them, and we are His church, His dwelling place on the earth. Amen.

I Pray

The Holy Spirit tells us of the urgency of prayer. God has made mankind wonderful, but our physical bodies are limited and can only take us so far. Prayer moves us beyond limitation; therefore, we must do as God says, pray. Amen.

I pray, dear Father. Early in my day, I seek You; I surrender all to You. Father, help me in every way, heal me and mine through and through, covering all the parts of our bodies. Please, Father, go before me, arrange my day, order my steps, and may You visit me in the cool of the day so that I might indulge in Your presence, fulfilling all of my needs according to Your riches, in glory by Christ Jesus. Father, may You give Your angels charge over me and mine, to keep us in the way we must go. May Your angels encamp round about us to protect us from our enemies. In my day, may it be ordained for my good and Your glory, and may my service to You prosper. Thank You, Father, for hearing me in Jesus' name. Amen.

Golden Nuggets

- In life, we may fall sometimes and may need help getting back up, but the good thing that comes out of falling is we can get back up, having insight that staying down is not an option.

- We realize through faith in Jesus; we have protection from God's blood against the consequences of sin.

"No One Lives or Dies to Himself"

For none of us liveth to himself, and no man dieth to himself. For where we live, we live unto the Lord; and whether we die, we die unto the Lord: whether we live therefore, or die, we are the Lord's. For to this end Christ both died, and rose, and revived, that he might be Lord both of the dead and living.

Romans 14:7–9

Chapter 20

The Word (In My Mind's Eyes)

On Saturday, March 7th, 2020, as I was worshiping the Lord our God that morning, scriptures started to go across my mind as if I was watching a movie. Not only did I see scriptures, but I also saw a wall of glass break in front of me, the pieces of glass appeared to fall from up to down. They were first shattered in the air, then fell in slow motion. For a minute or so, I got a chance to see them in the air, an amazing sight while I was praising God, listening to the songs "Order My Steps in Your Word" and "Now Behold the Lamb" by Kirk Franklin. We will go into detail at the end about this vision from God.

For the past week or so, the Holy Spirit has brought me back to the Word—"the Word of God," the Holy Spirit said to write. I'm thinking back to the week of February 28th, 2020, which was on a Friday after work. I was on my way to Jamaica Avenue to go to a store that sells hair products, and I was on the train with Mrs. B., a dear friend, a co-worker, and a pastor. While on the train, I happened to close my eyes for two to five minutes or so, and she asked me if I was okay. I, at first, did not know where to start, but the Holy Spirit said to tell her my revelation. I opened my eyes and smiled and said the Lord was showing me something in the spirit world about His Word. He gave me revelation knowledge about His Word, and I saw, in the spirit, through my spiritual eyes, every Word of God. The Word of God is not just groups of letters put together, but as it is spoken from your tongue, you are releasing the very Spirit of God into the atmosphere, and the Spirit of God is a living being. I saw the light in the figure of a person, but I could not make out the details of the face; the shape was in the form of a well-fit man—a spiritual body—and it seemed to have formed from out of my mouth into this created body.

That is about all I mentioned to her at that time, but it was then that I received a whole new way of understanding God's Word. I was seeing the same Word of God very differently and also receiving a mental picture/download during that day and being led to visit many scriptures as the Holy Spirit spoke through me God's Word. "For the word of God is quick, and powerful, and sharper than any two-edged sword, piercing even to the dividing asunder of soul and spirit, and of the joints and marrow, and is a discerner of the thoughts and intents of the heart" (Hebrews 4:12). "It is the spirit that quickeneth; the flesh profiteth nothing: the words that I speak unto you, they are spirit, and they are life" (John 6:63). "All scripture is given by inspiration of God, and is profitable for doctrine, for reproof, for correction, for instruction in righteousness: that the man of God may be perfect, thoroughly furnished unto all good works" (2 Timothy 3:16–17). "Is not my word like as a fire? Saith the Lord; and like a hammer that breaketh the rock in pieces" (Jeremiah 23:29)? "But he answered and said, It is written, Man shall not live by bread alone, but by every word that proceedeth out of the mouth of God" (Matthew 4:4). "The entrance of thy words giveth light; it giveth understanding unto the simple" (Psalm 119:130). "As for God, his way is perfect: the word of the Lord is tried: he is a buckler to all those that trust him" (Psalm 18:30). "In the beginning was the Word, and the Word was with God, and the Word was God" (John 1:1). "And the Word was made flesh, and dwelt among us, (and we beheld his glory, the glory as of the only begotten of the Father,) full of grace and truth" (John 1:14). "Who being the brightness of his glory, and the express image of his person, and upholding all things by the word of his power, when he had by himself purged our sins, sat down on the right hand of the Majesty on high" (Hebrews 1:3). "Let not your heart be troubled: ye believe in God, believe also in me" (John 14:1). "He that believeth on me, as the scripture

hath said, out of his belly shall flow rivers of living water" (John 7:38). "For the Lord giveth wisdom: out of his
mouth cometh knowledge and understanding" (Proverbs
2:6). "My Word and I are One; "It is the spirit that quickeneth; the flesh profiteth nothing: the words that I speak
unto you, they are spirit, and they are life" (John 6:63).

Going back to the beginning of this writing, "the Word"
in my mind's eyes, I saw and knew through my spiritual
mind/eyes pictures in the form of energy, which appeared
to be electrical energy, having a form of a man but no
recognizable features, and this electrical energy formed
went forth from the Word of God, which came from out
of my mouth, which was spoken from my tongue, into the
atmosphere and the spiritual world, with power from up
high, and God said it should not return void unto Him.
Amen. "Let every soul be subject unto the higher powers.
For there is no power but of God: the powers that be are
ordained of God" (Romans 13:1). As the scripture states,
what God has said, "So shall my word be that goeth forth
out of my mouth: it shall not return unto me void, but it
shall accomplish that which I please, and it shall prosper
in the thing whereto I sent it" (Isaiah 55:11).

> In that, I command thee this day to love the
> Lord thy God, to walk in his ways, and to

keep his commandments and his statutes and his judgments, that thou mayest live and multiply: and the Lord thy God shall bless thee in the land whither thou goest to possess it. That thou mayest love the Lord thy God, and that thou mayest obey his voice, and that thou mayest cleave unto him: for he is thy life, and the length of thy days: that thou mayest dwell in the land which the Lord sware unto thy fathers, to Abraham, to Isaac, and to Jacob, to give them.

Deuteronomy 30:16, 20

"Death and life are in the power of the tongue: and they that love it shall eat the fruit thereof" (Proverbs 18:21). "And the tongue is a fire, a world of iniquity: so is the tongue among our members, that it defileth the whole body, and setteth on fire the course of nature; and it is set on fire of hell" (James 3:6). In understanding from the Word above, likewise let us pray, "Let the words of my mouth, and the meditation of my heart, be acceptable in thy sight, O Lord, my strength, and my redeemer" (Psalm 19:14). It is good for us to meditate on God's Word. He assures us and says about His Word, "So shall my word be that goeth forth out of my mouth: it shall not return unto me void, but it shall accomplish that which I please, and it shall prosper in the thing whereto I sent it" (Isaiah 55:11). "And Jesus said unto them, Because of your unbelief: for verily I say unto you, If ye have faith as a grain of mustard seed, ye shall say unto this mountain, Remove hence to yonder place; and it shall remove; and nothing shall be impossible unto you" (Matthew 17:20). "For verily I say unto you, That whosoever shall say unto this mountain, Be thou removed, and be thou cast into the sea; and shall not doubt in his heart, but shall believe that those things which he saith shall come to pass; he shall have whatsoever he saith" (Mark 11:23). "For I say, through the grace given unto me, to every man that is among you, not to think of himself more highly than he ought to think; but to think soberly, according as God hath dealt to every man the measure of faith" (Romans 12:3). "If ye abide in me, and my words abide in you, ye shall ask what ye will, and it shall be done unto you" (John 15:7). "These things have I spoken unto you, that my joy might remain in you, and that your joy might be full" (John 15:11). Amen.

So Why Did God Allow Me to See the Shattered Wall Made Out of Thick Glass?

This vision represents the barrier between mankind and God. God wants every man and woman to shatter (break) the wall down that is between mankind and God by using the Word of God. Until the Holy Spirit is given, the Word is the only way mankind is able to hear from God. The Word of God is Jesus Christ, and to follow Him is the way, the truth, and life itself. Amen. God has not hidden the truth; you must seek after Him. To everyone, God has already given you a measure of faith, which holds the power to choose, and no one can take it from you. God has given this to you so that you also may be with Him. Amen. To those who are blessed to read this, I have seen the Word of God in the spirit and (tears are forming in my eyes as I am sharing this), the Word of God is not only majestic "but mighty through God to the pulling down of strongholds," and this is the scripture given to me for my youngest son when he was around four years of age by the Holy Spirit, to give him comfort as he slept through the night, and this is his testimony if he chooses to share one day. I will say this scripture, like all the others, works and does for the glory of God, amen. "For the weapons of our warfare are not carnal, but mighty through God to the pulling down of strongholds; Casting down imaginations, and every high thing that exalteth itself against the knowledge of God, and bringing into captivity every thought to the obedience of Christ" (2 Corinthians 10:4–5). God alerts us to the things that come against us that are spiritual. "For we wrestle not against flesh and blood, but against principalities, against powers, against the rulers of the darkness of this world, against spiritual wickedness in high places" (Ephesians 6:12).

I've been comforted in the arms and the bosom of God; I have been slowly, carefully, and lovingly put back together after being broken into pieces spiritually. I've been made whole by the hands of God; I have been hidden in the secret place of the Most High God, from principalities in high places. I have witnessed miracles, and I know not to take that lightly. To mention a few miracles I have seen, by Jesus' stripes, healings, including one healed totally from terminal cancer, and countless more. The Holy Spirit reminds me to mention the miracle He gave to my oldest son. Weeks before it happened, because of the continuous visions and dreams I had beforehand, I was filled with terror of what I had seen in them. I had even spoken with a dear friend, Mrs. B, about them. I rebuked the visions and dreams because I did not believe that it was God's will, but little did I know it had to happen, and God was preparing me for it. Then it happened, what I had prayed against for weeks. It was a hot day; my son had just gotten in. I was off this day, and I was sitting in the living room where the AC was. My son wanted to adjust the temperature control on the air conditioner; I was cold from sitting under it for a while, watching television. I asked him to come back and adjust it to the temperature he needed in fifteen minutes or so. I had heard a great big boom not too long after the fifteen minutes had passed; I ignored it because I thought it was the children next door throwing a basketball against the wall, as they sometimes do. I called out to my son to adjust the AC so his room would get more air, but there was no answer. I waited and called out again, no answer. All of a sudden, I felt the urge to go and look for him. About that time, a gentle voice said, "He was supposed to change the temperature by now," then, the shawl I had over my shoulder became heated up like fire, and I threw the shawl off of me and heard again the voice say, "Go see about him now!"

When I knocked on the bathroom door, there was no answer; when I tried to open the door, the door was blocked. I could not open the door because my oldest son was laid out on the floor, his body stiff, and he was unresponsive. I found him not breathing, and he was dark in color and without a pulse for almost an hour. To make a long tragedy short, God raised my oldest son from death because God had said to me that He gave me resurrection faith for this son of mine. As tears of overwhelming gratitude stir up in my eyes because of countless miracles I have witnessed and storms God has brought me through, I have come to the conclusion that there are no earthly words that can properly describe the magnitude of the Word of God—how powerful God's Word is. The love of God towards us, how true it is, and seeing God's Word in the spirit at work clarifies again any doubts that I might have had, or I might have, concerning prayers, about being answered by God in a timely manner and so much more.

Just to mention, after God gave me resurrection faith for this son of mine, I'm not telling my oldest son's entire testimony but sharing this truth. Know that there were many essential workers—the firemen and the ambulance workers, it must have been ten (10) or more people in my living room. As I remember with all the things I had in my living room, I'm not sure how they all fit, but what God showed me afterward was that His angels were there also, as witnesses. They seemed to have vanished soon after. To continue, while in the ambulance on the way to the hospital to further check out how my son was doing internally, the medical team in the ambulance repeatedly told my son how he was given a miracle and that he should be thankful for surviving and thankful for being alert after being dead for almost an hour. When we finally arrived at the hospital, the doctor said he could not find anything wrong from the tragedy, so we got to come home immediately. Let us take a look at the word miracle: miracles—we believe are divine intervention. The Holy Spirit calls divine intervention answers to prayers given by God to those with a pure heart towards God and a right spirit towards Him. My heart and soul magnify the Lord. I thank God, for He is good. He continues to answer my prayers. Amen.

Golden Nuggets

- Daughter/Son, I am the Lord your God who does not bring tribulation/suffering upon you, though at times, I may allow it. Know this, if I do not allow you to go through an impossible situation, then how would you know that I am the God who can do impossible things? If I had not allowed you to be in a situation where you need a miracle, how then would you know that I am the God of miracles? Amen. I will pray, "Create in me a clean heart, O God; and renew a right spirit within me" (Psalm 51:10). Amen.

- Concerning my children and me, when death sorted out to enslave us, God said, "Death, you are out of line," and made old man death behave! God also said that my children and I are His, telling death to release us, saying, "They are mine!" It could have been me and my children captured by old man death, but Jesus, because of His mercy and the price He had paid for our freedom, by God's grace, God decided to remind me and death about that, amen.

"Observe Each Day to the Lord"

One man esteemeth one day above another: another esteemeth every day alike. Let every man be fully persuaded in his own mind. He that regardeth the day, regardeth it unto the Lord; and he that regardeth not the day, to the Lord he doth not regard it. He that eateth, eateth to the Lord, for he giveth God thanks; and he that eateth not, to the Lord he eateth not, and giveth God thanks.

Romans 14:5–6

Chapter 21

Your Words

Words are like seeds; once released from you, they become planted, waiting for the most opportune time (right conditions) to grow. There is both a good seed (words) and an evil seed (words) that do exist. Depending on what seed you plant (which comes from your tongue), it will determine what springs forth. In other words, say what you'd like to see grow and not what you do not want to appear/ spring forth. Please remember this; there is a spirit behind each word: God's Word, God's Spirit. For evil words, demonic spirits, there is no middle ground. Therefore, since God knows best and more than we do, it is always in our best interest to do as He says. God is very straightforward about what we should say and warns us, "Wherefore laying aside all malice, and all guile, and hypocrisies, and envies, and all evil speakings" (1 Peter 2:1). "Let no corrupt communication proceed out of your mouth, but that which is good to the use of edifying, that it may minister grace unto the hearers" (Ephesians 4:29). "Death and life are in the power of the tongue: and they that love it shall eat the fruit thereof" (Proverbs 18:21). "Whoso keepeth his mouth and his tongue keepeth his soul from troubles" (Proverbs 21:23). "But I say unto you, That every idle word that men shall speak, they shall give account thereof in the day of judgment. For by thy words thou shalt be justified, and by the words, thou shalt be condemned" (Matthew 12:36–37). Amen.

Golden Nugget

- The Holy Spirit says, If you want to take a peek into your future, just pay attention to these truths: what comes from your tongue (what you say)? What do you think about often, how you spend your time, what you study, and who you associate with (hang around)? By knowing these things, which are stated above, we can expect, more or less, what will show up in our future; we also have a chance to make better choices by knowing these truths.

Chapter 22

Words

Words are given by God; they carry unimaginable power. Words spoken have the authority to break barriers between time and eternity. Words are incredibly divine. Words can summon things. Words are creative. I know all the above to be true, and this is why God wants us to be careful to guard our tongues at all times. "Even so the tongue is a little member, and boasteth great things. Behold, how great a matter a little fire kindleth" (James 3:5)! "Out of the same mouth proceedeth blessing and cursing. My brethren, these things ought not so be. Doth a fountain send forth at the same place sweet water and bitter" (James 3:10–11)? "Thy tongue deviseth mischiefs; like a sharp razor, working deceitfully" (Psalm 52:2). "Thou art snared with the words of thy mouth, thou art taken with the words of thy mouth" (Proverbs 6:2). "Not that which goeth into the mouth defileth a man; but that which cometh out of the mouth, this defileth a man" (Matthew 15:11). "There is that speaketh like the piercings of a sword: but the tongue of the wise is health" (Proverbs 12:18). "A wholesome tongue is a tree of life: but perverseness therein is a breach in the spirit" (Proverbs 15:4). "The Lord shall cut off flattering lips, and the tongue that speaketh proud things" (Psalm 12:3). "Keep thy tongue from evil, and thy lips from speaking guile" (Psalm 34:13). I will pray, "Deliver my soul, O Lord, from lying lips, and from a deceitful tongue" (Psalm 120:2). "Set a watch, O Lord, before my mouth; keep the door of my lips" (Psalm 141:3). Amen.

Golden Nuggets

- Words are powerful; one word has the potential to create many out of it; a word has creative power. Each word is full of life, just as a tiny seed. To me, words are like seeds, and once spoken, they are released and immediately grow wherever planted. Once that word takes root, it is as powerful as dynamite. Some words blossom, and some words explode.

- "Even as I have seen, they that plow iniquity, and sow wickedness, reap the same" (Job 4:8).

- It is important for us to know that we must say what we mean and not what we don't mean.

- It is good, therefore, to imitate God. We must remember one word from God changes everything. When we speak, let's plant seeds/words that blossom beautifully. Oh Lord, may I have Your guidance, "Let the words of my mouth, and the meditation of my heart, be acceptable in thy sight, O Lord, my strength, and my redeemer" (Psalm 19:14). Amen.

"Guard Your Tongue"

"Whoso keepeth his mouth and his tongue keepeth his soul from troubles" (Proverbs 21:23).

Chapter 23

Talking to Our Father in Heaven

Father and Lord, these are the things I know: I can never get enough of being in the presence of Your love, I can never stop praising You, I would never find greater joy because it's only found in You. Your peace surpasses all understanding. There is no God greater than You. You sent Jesus; I know Your love is true. I can search heaven and earth, and there would never be another You that could love me as You do. You have given me countless blessings, and I am very grateful to know Your love. You love me even when I struggle to love myself. Father, I need Your help; I want to bring You glory. I know I can never do it by myself. When I give thanks to You, I know it's not enough. If you are willing, Father, help me; I want to go all out for You because You went all out for me by giving us Your Son (Jesus). My soul sings and magnifies You, Lord. Eternally, amen.

Golden Nugget

- Do not give up on yourself because God, our Creator who created heaven and earth, has not given up on you. This is why He sent Jesus. Trust in God in all things, and He is faithful to guide you through. Let us pray. Lord God, I trust in You, help our words to be benefiting to others as well as to ourselves for Your Glory. In Jesus' name, amen.

Chapter 24

My Spirit Magnifies the Lord

There is nobody like You, Lord! No one can compare to You! No one besides You, only You! You are my Healer, Lord! You are the miracle worker! You are my Savior, Lord! You are the Redeemer! No one is as great as You! No one can even come close to You! You have no equal! You are holy! You are awesome! Everything must bow to You! Your Name is above every name! Your Spirit is unmatched! You are One God, but yet Three Persons! The earth testifies of Your glory! The heavens testify to Your majesty! Eternity bows down to Your every word! There is no word that explains Your candor! My heart cries out in awe of You! You are amazing! You are the air I breathe, Alleluia! My heart cries out—You are great! And my life testifies that You alone are good. Amen. "The heavens declare the glory of God, and the firmament sheweth his handiwork" (Psalm 19:1).

Bless God! Amen.

Golden Nugget

- Know that if one is bound to sin, he is not free to praise God and, therefore, is unable to enjoy the blessings which come from his praise to God, amen. "O Lord thou art my God; I will exalt thee, I will praise thy name; for thou hast done wonderful things; thy counsels of old are faithfulness and truth" (Isaiah 25:1). My Lord and my God, how You love us, thank You for loving me; I know I will never find a love like Yours outside of Your love; the love that does exist will never measure up. "Bless the Lord, O my soul: and all that is within me, bless his holy name" (Psalm 103:1). "Let everything that hath breath praise the Lord. Praise ye the Lord" (Psalm 150:6). Amen.

Chapter 25

The Spiritual Body

Let us revisit some truths about the spiritual and the physical body. Did you know that the spiritual body moves at a completely different speed than the physical body? Your spiritual body moves so much faster/swiftly than your physical body; even while being perfectly still, you can still break a sweat, meaning the physical body has to work hard just to keep up with the spiritual body without you noticing it. For example, I can tell you something you might know about already, but I will not talk about the details of the added information given to me by the Holy Spirit of God because I know it will take a long time to explain.

What I am about to share with you is from personal awareness (in a dream). To continue with the example, we all know about dreams, but did you know that some dreams are true and are happening in the spirit realm or that they will happen sometime in the future? That is another story we will not get into right now. The Holy Spirit wants me to point out that in some dreams, when you are physically asleep, and there is no movement except breathing, the world calls this REM sleep. Furthermore, when you are dreaming, your spiritual body—you might see yourself running in your dream, and when you wake up, you are sweaty from perspiring while sleeping. Our spiritual body and physical body are somehow connected to one another. Your spiritual body moves faster or at a different speed than your physical. If we fast, maybe skip breakfast or lunch and pray, then fill up (renew our mind) with the Word of God/the Scriptures from the Holy Bible and believe you will then have fed your spiritual body, and it will increase with power from God in all kinds of ways unimaginable, even while awake. Your life will change for the better. The spiritual body can exist outside of your physical body. Know this to be under the guidance of the Holy Spirit of God, and you do not grieve Him: you are protected from evil, amen. "And grieve not the Holy Spirit of God, whereby ye are sealed unto the day of redemption (Ephesians 4:30). "For I long to see you, that I may impart unto you some spiritual gift, to the end ye may be established" (Romans 1:11). "Now concerning spiritual gifts, brethren, I would not have you ignorant" (1 Corinthians 12:1). "I knew a man in Christ above fourteen years ago, (whether in the body, I cannot tell; or whether out of the body, I cannot tell: God knoweth;) such an one caught up to the third heaven" (2 Corinthians 12:2).

In other words, God has allowed me to know that the spiritual body can move around outside of your physical body; he can go back and forth into eternity while your physical body still breathes (while you are alive), that you can go where God is now. "And hath raised us up together, and made us sit together in heavenly places in Christ Jesus" (Ephesians 2:6). For those who are believers of Jesus Christ, we can sit in heavenly places as is stated above. God says one thing we must do is never give place to the devil, meaning we must guard our heart against anything that is against God, so we are not giving access to the devil to do as he pleases in us. Amen.

How Do We Do This?

The Holy Spirit says we must live by every Word of God, we must pursue peace within ourselves, and we must pray always. "Depart from evil, and do good; seek peace, and pursue it" (Psalm 34:14). "Let him eschew evil, and do good; let him seek peace, and ensue it" (1 Peter 3:11). "These things I have spoken unto you, that in me ye might have peace. In the world ye shall have tribulation: but be of good cheer; I have overcome the world" (John 16:33). "Deceit is in the heart of them that imagine evil: but to the counsellors of peace is joy" (Proverbs 12:20). "Follow peace with all men, and holiness without which no man shall see the Lord" (Hebrews 12:14).

Why Does God Say, Be Holy?

The Holy Spirit instructs me that to be holy is to be sanctified for God, to not be a part of sin, and to stay away from whatever is against God. Holiness helps us to obey God. Holiness keeps us from following after sin. Holiness limits the power of Satan's attacks against us. Holiness is a commandment from God because holiness is purposed for our good; therefore, we must be holy as God says. I will say that God Himself, He and His Word, is holy, and holiness is more than enough for anyone to receive, but nevertheless, we should receive anyway because God commands that we be holy as He is. Amen.

Golden Nuggets

- In every human being, within you, there is a place God Himself has placed that He alone can fill. Mankind is not complete until he or she has truly accepted/surrendered to God. God cannot be ignored or dismissed. You too will know that God exists once you enter His Shekinah Glory, you will not be able to deny that He is who He says He is, the One True and Almighty God (God in Three Persons—Triune) who lives, was dead, and lives forevermore, amen.

- The world may give you happiness, but it cannot last, and the end thereof will always lead to sorrow; always know that the joy from God is endless, and there is no sorrow in it, ever, says the Holy Spirit, amen. God speaks, "I am he that liveth, and was dead; and, behold, I am alive forevermore, Amen" (Revelation 1:18). I will say, "Thou art worthy, O Lord, to receive glory and honour and power: for thou hast created all things, and for thy pleasure, they are and were created" (Revelation 4:11).

Amen.

God Prepares Heaven for Us!

Let not your heart be troubled: ye believe in God, believe also in me. In my Father's house are many mansions: if it were not so, I would have told you. I go to prepare a place for you. And if I go and prepare a place for you, I will come again, and receive you unto myself; that where I am, there ye may be also. And whither I go ye know, and the way ye know.

John 14:1–4

Amen.

My God and Lord, "When thou saidst, Seek ye my face; my heart said unto thee, Thy face, Lord, will I seek. I had fainted, unless I had believed to see the goodness of the Lord in the land of the living" (Psalm 27:8, 13).

The Holy Spirit says, "God has given us so much, and if you really want to know Him, God says, 'Get wisdom, get understanding: forget it not; neither decline from the words of my mouth'" (Proverbs 4:5). Amen

THE *Kingdom* OF *God* IS AT *Hand*

God says, "It is essential that we, 'Pray without ceasing'" (1 Thessalonians 5:17).

Let's find out why, as God powerfully explains in book 2.

9 781685 564469